THE FOUNTAINWELL DRAMA TEXTS

22

GEORGE FARQUHAR

THE RECRUITING OFFICER

Edited by

A. NORMAN JEFFARES

To Ken and Angela from Derry with all good wishes as ever [illegible] 92

OLIVER & BOYD
EDINBURGH
1973

OLIVER AND BOYD
Croythorn House
23 Ravelston Terrace
Edinburgh, EH4 3TJ

A Division of Longman Group Limited

First Published 1973

0 05 002697 6 Hardback
0 05 002696 8 Paperback

Printed in Great Britain by
Cox & Wyman Ltd
London, Fakenham and Reading

ACKNOWLEDGMENTS

For assistance and advice in the preparation of this edition I am greatly indebted to my colleagues Mr John Horden and Mr Brian Scobie.

A. N. J.

CONTENTS

CRITICAL INTRODUCTION

I THE PLAY

In 1705 George Farquhar, commissioned as a Lieutenant of Grenadiers the year before in Lord Orrery's regiment of foot, was sent on a recruiting trip to Lichfield and Shrewsbury. The Irish playwright had, reputedly, at the age of thirteen, taken part in the Battle of the Boyne in 1690 "under Colonel Hamilton", so he may have had a predilection for military life. He certainly enjoyed his recruiting experiences, and Lord Orrery commented on his great diligence in this occupation, regarding him as "very Serviceable both in Raising and Recruiting ye sd. Reigmt".[1] Out of memories of his stay in Lichfield Farquhar was to create *The Beaux Stratagem* when he was dying in 1706 at the age of thirty, but he began *The Recruiting Officer* when he was still in Shrewsbury in 1705, completing at least the draft and probably the whole of the play there. He dedicated it "To all Friends round the Wrekin", a steep hill outside Shrewsbury. It was approved by the Duke of Ormonde and by Lord Orrery, who were both engaged in exercises in the area. Farquhar had finished the comedy by 12 February 1706 and gave the manuscript to Bernard Lintot in Fleet Street, receiving £16 *2s. 6d.* as an advance. It was first performed at Drury Lane on 8 April 1706 and was enormously successful, seven further performances being given that April, three of them, on 10, 15 and 20 April, for the author's benefit. The cast included Wilks as Captain Plume, Cibber as Captain Brazen, and Eastcourt as Serjeant Kite, while Anne Oldfield played Silvia. The play was repeated in June; a gala performance took place in Bath in October; and the Drury Lane Company played it for their re-opening at Dorset Gardens on 24 October. After most of the Drury Lane actors had gone over to the Haymarket in the autumn of 1706 the play was staged there by Swiney on the same nights in November as Rich played it with the remains of his company now back in Drury Lane.[2]

[1] Quoted by James Sutherland, "New Light on George Farquhar", *Times Literary Supplement*, 6 March 1937, p. 371.

[2] See Sybil Rosenfeld, "Notes on *The Recruiting Officer*", *Theatre Notebook* XVIII, Winter 1963–4, 47–48.

Lintot published the first quarto of the play on 12 April 1706, four days after the highly successful first performance. In the Dedication of the play, Farquhar remarked that the entertainment he found in Shropshire commanded him to be grateful. His period of recruiting had gone pleasantly and well there, though he probably spent too much of his money on it in the hope of promotion. He had made friendships with the local Justices and country gentry, and he liked the people and the place. Both provided much of the material for his play, "some little turns of humour", he remarked, that he met with "almost within the shade of that famous hill", the Wrekin, gave rise to his comedy. Some of the Salopians were anxious lest he should ridicule the country gentlemen when back in London, but he reassured them that he was writing a comedy not a libel, and that no one from that area could suffer from being exposed while he "held to nature". He had found that recruiting in Shrewsbury was the greatest pleasure in the world to him: "The Kingdom could not show better bodies of men, better inclinations for the service, more generosity, more good understanding, nor more politeness than is to be found at the foot of the Wrekin."

The characters were based on living originals. E. Blakeway wrote to Bishop Percy, on 4 July 1765, that an old lady in Shrewsbury remembered that Farquhar remained on his recruiting tour in the town long enough to write his play, and she identified the characters as follows:

> Justice Balance is Mr Berkley then Deputy Recorder of the town—One of the other Justices, a Mr Hill, an inhabitant of Shrewsbury—Mr Worthy is Mr Owen of Rusason on the borders of Shropshire—Captn Plume is Farquhar himself—Brazen unknown—Melinda is Miss [Dorothy] Harnage of Belsadine near the Wrekin—Sylvia, Miss [Laconia] Berkley Daughter of the Recorder above mentioned. The story I suppose the Poets invention.[1]

Jones, who accompanied Farquhar on his recruiting tour, provided a model for Sergeant Kite, while Farquhar obviously put a great deal of his own personality into Captain Plume, dashing, lively, impressionable and, ultimately, serious. Plume explains himself to the supposed Jack Wilful:

[1] Quoted by Charles Stonehill (ed.) *The Complete Works of George Farquhar* (1930), p. xxvi.

> No, Faith, I am not that Rake that the World imagines, I have got an Air of Freedom which People mistake for Lewdness in me as they mistake Formality in others for Religion; the World is all a Cheat, only I take mine which is undesign'd to be more excusable than theirs, which is hypocritical; I hurt nobody but my self, but they abuse all Mankind.

Brazen was probably a mixture of the stock *miles gloriosus* character, of aspects of Farquhar's fellow-officers, and of various foppish characters in Restoration drama. He does, however, gain Plume's recruits at the end of the play, and so may be regarded as an efficient recruiting officer.

There were, of course, literary sources. Farquhar's own play *The Stage-Coach* (1704), founded on Jean de la Chapelle's *Les Carosses d'Orleans*, had shown him the dramatic advantages of observing the unities, and had also taught him the advantages of placing his action in the country rather than the town, and of avoiding the stereotyped plots of the Restoration wits. In his own *The Twin Rivals* he had used the idea of two couples. And he owed much to his study of Ben Jonson, to whom he paid tribute in the preface to *The Stage-Coach*. Willard Connely has argued[1] that Kite's haranguing manner came from the opening scene of the second act of *Volpone* (where Volpone, disguised as a mountebank doctor, sets up to sell his remedies to the crowd), though Farquhar, who particularly appreciated the "rich gifts of Nature" in Jonson, made Kite's speeches more natural.

The plot revolves around the recruiting of rustics and the love affairs of Captain Plume, Captain Brazen, Worthy and the two girls Silvia and Melinda. Sergeant Kite, masquerading as an astrologer, and possibly based on Congreve's character Foresight in *Love for Love*, becomes a king-pin in the action, and the Justices aid the recruiting and, less wittingly, one of the love affairs.

The main lines of the plot are not very complex. The first act opens with Sergeant Kite trying to recruit grenadiers. The local bumpkins are suspicious of him, but learn to take advantage of his offer of ale. Kite confers with Plume and thus we learn, in a dialogue which is highly amusing on stage, of the birth of Plume's bastard, of Kite's five marriages, and of the enlisting of Plume's child. This establishes the play's parallels between military and civilian life; for war, as Ballance

[1] See Connely, *Young George Farquhar* (1949), pp. 243–4.

later points out, is the soldier's mistress; begetting bastards is another form of recruiting. We also hear of Kite's fortune-telling disguise, and next, on Worthy's entry, we hear of his so far unsuccessful pursuit of Melinda, who has inherited twenty thousand pounds and become affected. Plume, for his part, loves Silvia but remarks that he is resolved never to bind himself to a woman for his whole life till he knows whether he will like her company for half an hour:

> . . . if People wou'd but try one another's Constitutions before they engag'd, it would prevent all these Elopements, Divorces and the Devil knows what.

Silvia's character is then explained. She would have the wedding before consummation while Plume was for consummation before the wedding: yet he admires her frank, generous disposition. Indeed Silvia has given money to the mother of Plume's child and sent word to her that the child will be taken care of; she has also sent a message that her father, Justice Ballance, would like to see Plume. Silvia is unlike Melinda, who is inclined to coquet with everyone she sees, and Worthy fears that Captain Brazen, the other recruiting captain, may be his rival for her affections. Both Silvia and Worthy are whole-hearted lovers, and Silvia's viewpoint rather than Melinda's is the one with which we are meant to sympathise.

The play continues to develop the differences between Silvia and Melinda in the second scene of the first Act. Silvia is a "natural" woman with the constitution of a horse: able to "gallop all the Morning after the Hunting Horn and all the Evening after a Fiddle", she is untroubled by "neither Spleen, Cholick nor Vapours". Melinda, however, is affected in her treatment of Worthy, for whereas Silvia does not like a man with confirmed thoughts and regards constancy as but a dull sleepy quality at best, Melinda thinks the worse of Worthy for associating with Plume.

Plume's character, however, is not as depraved as Melinda's words might suggest. In the opening of the second act there is a frank discussion between Justice Ballance and Plume, in which Plume assures him he has no designs on Silvia. He tells Silvia herself that he has made her his heir and in her generosity and determination not to be possessive or censorious she remarks that he should have left something to his child. Later in the fourth act Plume explains to Silvia (then disguised as Mr Wilful) that he is "not that Rake that the World imagines". He has an air of freedom which people mistake for lewdness. Unlike those who mistake formality for religion, he is no hypocrite. He talks briefly about his recruiting methods.

These we have seen in action earlier in the play. Plume and Kite work well together. When Kite has planted his gold pieces (he was only paying the equivalent of twenty three shillings and sixpence, whereas according to the relevant Acts of Parliament the sum should have been twenty shillings for each person recruited. Plume's two guineas was more correct, as volunteers were paid forty shillings) Plume affects to drive him off and the men enlist in admiration of Plume's apparent championing of their cause. Again, he works very successfully through the agency of Rose. And Kite, as supposed astrologer and fortune-teller, sets up situations through which Plume will be able to recruit the credulous visitors to the astrologer. (In this role Kite also continues to bring Melissa and Worthy together.) Plume's generosity appears later in the play when Justice Ballance, realising Silvia's disguise as Wilful and suspecting this is a plot of Plume's, offers to buy the supposed young man out of the army. He is freely given the discharge by Plume who, ignorant of Wilful's true identity, values the Justice's friendship too much to make money out of him. Plume is not, of course, committed to his recruiting trade, and at the play's end is happily ready to settle down to the life of a country gentleman, offering Brazen the twenty recruits he has collected.

The court scene where dishonesty reigns offers the audience, beyond its pure comedy, the chance to realise that some of those who are impressed do not deserve its pity. For instance, the man who pretends to support five children is enlisted because he is a poacher. The collier who pretends to be married is accused by Kite of having no visible means of livelihood because he works underground: but his supposed wife clinches this dubious argument in favour of his enlistment by revealing that they had agreed she should call him husband to avoid passing for a whore and that he should call her wife "to shun going for a soldier". The dishonesty of the constable is shown when Silvia is brought into court; and he is then taken into custody by Kite, to be held until his friends have ransomed him with four recruits.

A bald account of the plot of *The Recruiting Officer* could hardly convey the speed of its action, the involved interweaving of the recruiting and the three love affairs. Indeed Farquhar probably wrote the play quickly, and was himself entangled enough in it to have made some mistakes.[1] For instance, Silvia calls herself Jack Wilful in III, ii when Plume enlists her, and she is known by this name in IV, ii, but in V, ii when she is first brought into court she calls herself Captain Pinch. When she is brought in again, she is called Pinch by her father and Plume, who is now present, makes no objection when she is enlisted as Pinch. We might argue that Plume would tolerate a pseudonym, as he tolerated Silvia's supposed conquest of Rose, but it seems that Farquhar either didn't develop this idea or else forgot that Plume knew her previously only by the name of Wilful. The latter seems probable since in V, vii Ballance sends for Silvia as Mr Wilful though previously he has only known her in court as Pinch. Another inconsistency is that Lucy has been writing in her own hand to Captain Brazen (in the hopes of marrying him) but signing her letters Melinda. But she uses Melinda's signature (which she steals—"I'll secure one copy for my own Affairs"—at the fortune-teller's in IV, ii) when she writes to Brazen to arrange a place of meeting whence they can elope. She runs the risk, and for no apparent reason, Brazen may realise that the signature has changed. The dramatic purpose behind this is, of course, that Plume shall recognise this signature as genuinely Melinda's when Brazen shows it to him and report this to Worthy, who will regard the elopement of Brazen and Melinda as genuine, rush to interrupt it and thus ruin Lucy's plot of trapping Brazen into marrying her. Again, the first and second bumpkins are Costar and Thummas respectively when they appear in the second act; but at the end of the act they give their names as Thummas Appletree and Costar Pearmain.[2]

The main action of the play centres on the recruiting drive. Farquhar presents recruiting as it was. In the process we learn how soldiers were recruited for the war of the Spanish Succession. There were many ways of using and abusing the Mutiny and Impressment Acts of 1703, 1704, and 1706, and the Justices of the Peace could put able-bodied men into the armed forces if they were deemed to have no lawful calling or occupation, or no visible means of support. The court scene in the play, the antics of Kite and the pressure exerted by Plume illustrate the power of the Justices, as well as the dishonesty of

[1] See Robert L. Hough, "An Error in 'The Recruiting Officer'" *N & Q*, CXCVIII, August 1953, pp. 340–41, and "Farquhar: 'The Recruiting Officer'" *N & Q* New Series 1, Nov. 1954, p. 454.

[2] See Eric Rothstein, *George Farquhar*. New York (Twayne Publishers, Inc.) 1967, p. 130.

both recruiters and those unwilling to be recruited. Plume is successful in his operation. Farquhar is not concerned to sermonise about Plume's methods (no doubt he acted similarly on his own campaign in Lichfield and Shrewsbury), nor does he provide socio-political comment on them. He is out to amuse, and he does this with a mixture of gaiety and tolerance; indeed Professor Rothstein has called the play "almost a comic documentary".[1]

Farquhar made use of Restoration devices in his comedy. There are echoes of Restoration bawdiness in plenty in the dialogue. The love affairs revolve around the finances of marriage and the choice of a socially suitable partner, as in most Restoration comedies. Kite's bogus-astrology reminds us of Congreve's *Love for Love*, and both Lucy's wearing a mask in her vain attempt to deceive Captain Brazen and her use of false letters, and even Silvia's pretending to be a young man have their models. The "breeches" part appealed to Farquhar; he had used it earlier, for Leanthe in *Love and a Bottle* (1698) and for Oriana in *The Inconstant* (1702). But he gave it a new turn with Silvia's pursuit of Plume, for she is a tolerant heroine; not unlike Sophia Western, she has grown up in the country, no milk and water Miss, but rather a new type of heroine, just as the play itself is a new kind of comedy. She can act the part of a gallant, she can be pert and witty; but she is lacking in feminine jealousy, in pride and in affectation, and is a "natural" woman.

The treatment of the rustics also reveals some natural kindness at work—in Bullock's clumsy protectiveness of his sister Rose, for instance. The same easiness appears in Plume's relationships with Ballance—the two men genuinely like each other—and Silvia wants to be brought to court so that her father will commit her (as "Jack Wilful") to Plume's care and thus authorise her escapade. Melinda is frightened by Kite into caring for Worthy—both Silvia and Lucy had urged her to this earlier—and it seems likely that she and Worthy, who lives up to his name, will make a success of marriage. Plume, of course, is not the gay libertine he might at first seem. He and Silvia have a liking for each other which is based on a tolerant attitude to life.

There is, then, a benignity in the drawing of the characters which marks the play off from other Restoration comedies, as well as a liveliness which came from Farquhar's portrayal of new themes: recruitment and country life. He is concerned to wed army and country

[1] Eric Rothstein, *George Farquhar*, p. 129.

together, and Silvia is the necessary link. Kenneth Tynan reports William Gaskill when producing as seeing three main actions or objectives in play: (1) Silvia's determination to get Plume (2) Plume's and Kite's determination to get recruits and (3) Worthy's determination to get Melinda. Gaskill saw (1) and (2) brought together by Silvia's male impersonation, while Brazen's designs on Melinda linked (1) and (3).[1]

There is no censorious attitude to the army, which reduces all matters to military parlance and situations. But civilian life provides analogies and sex is seen in martial terms. The two worlds need each other: the army defends the social order represented by Justice Ballance. The virtually stock characters illustrate Farquhar's view of what a harmonious, stable society could be, and he regarded the army as an essential part of it. The rustics have an energetic patriotic capacity, so have the Justices, especially Ballance, who is one of Farquhar's best creations. Both he and Plume play their parts in seeing that the army is supplied with recruits. The role of the army in society is underlined by Silvia's love for both her father and Plume: that she successfully deceives both is in the best traditions of comedy, and leads to an ideal solution in which Ballance regains a son and heir in the person of Plume, while Plume is deceived in order, ultimately, to win his wife. Silvia's actions lead also to the marriage of Melinda and Worthy, and to Brazen's success in recruiting.

II CRITICAL RECEPTION OF THE PLAY

Arthur Bedford's *The Evil and Danger of Stage Plays* (1706) contained an attack on *The Recruiting Officer*. He regarded the play as an attack on recruiting, and objected to the characterisations of the Captains as liars, drunkards and debauchers of women. They were quarrelsome and cowardly, and Kite was guilty of using profane language and in "Commendation of the Devil". John Oldmixon, a rival and enemy of Farquhar, was probably the author of a more charitable assessment of Farquhar's work which appeared in *The Muses Mercury*, May 1707, in which the author's two last plays—*The Recruiting Officer* and *The Beaux Stratagem*—were regarded as truly humorous and diverting. Though the critics would not allow any part of them to be

[1] See *The Recruiting Officer*, ed. K. Tynan, 1965, p. 16 where both he and Gaskill make unduly heavy weather of the court scene, and (unreasonably) blame Farquhar for failing to clarify Silvia's motives.

"regular", the article continued, Mr Farquhar had a genius for comedy: his plays possessed novelty and mirth in general and pleased the audiences whenever they were staged. The critic wrote almost as if he were baffled by Farquhar's success: "His conduct, though not artful, was surprising; his characters, though not great, were just; his humours, though low, diverting; his dialogue, though loose and incorrect, gay and agreeable; and his wit though not superabundant, pleasant."

Richard Steele, discussing *The Recruiting Officer* in the *Tatler* two years later on 20 May 1709, had somewhat similar reservations. He praised Eastcourt's acting; his

> proper Sense and Observation supports the Play. There is not in my humble opinion, the Humour but in Sergeant Kite; but it is admirably supply'd by his Action.

An Audience in Cork in September 1763 sharply resented the play's being cut, and the theatrical company was taken to task for this omission of a scene by the Cork *Evening Post*, 7 September 1763.

In *Biographica Dramatica* (1812) David Erskine was content to give an account of Farquhar's life rather than offer criticism of his work, and supplied an interesting comment on Farquhar as an undergraduate[1] at Trinity College, Dublin:

> The modes of study in that place being calculated rather for making deep than polite scholars, and Mr. Farquhar being totally averse to serious pursuits, he was reckoned by all his fellow students one of the dullest young men in the University and even as a companion he was thought extremely heavy and disagreeable.

Leigh Hunt in a discussion of *The Recruiting Officer* in 1818 thought Farquhar degraded sympathy into dissipation and left evil things evil, while Hazlitt in his *Lectures on the English Comic Writers* (1819) stated that English comedy began to decline from Farquhar's time. But he praised the truth and nature in Farquhar's comedies; he found the character in the plays full of life and spirit even though they were sometimes apparently left in an unfinished state. He liked the constant ebullition of "gay, laughing invention, cordial good humour and fine animal spirits" in Farquhar's writings; and he had no objection to Farquhar's heroines who forfeited appearances but saved their honour.

[1] See also Peter Kavanagh's letter, "George Farquhar", *The Times Literary Supplement*, 10 Feb. 1945, p. 72.

Charles Lamb in his essay "On the artificial comedy of the last century" in the *Essays of Elia* (1823) was more interested in putting forward the view that Restoration comedy was *sui generis* than in offering a full treatment of Farquhar's work. Campenon, the French critic who translated *The Recruiting Officer* in 1823, took a puritanical view of the play:

> En retractant la vie debaucheé de l'officier recruteur il n'a rien atténué, rien dissimulé dans cette peinture des moeurs licencieuses j'ai cru devoir souvent adoucir ses expressions, pour les rendre supportables à des oreilles françaises.

Edmund Gosse wrote a sympathetic biography of Farquhar in 1892 and gave a brief account of *The Recruiting Officer* in it: and he praised Farquhar as the last great dramatist of the Restoration in his *History of Eighteenth Century Literature* (1660–1780) seven years later. His edition of 1926 contained an appreciative note. Sir Adolphus Ward was less amiable in *A History of English Dramatic Literature* (new edition, 1899). He described *The Recruiting Officer* as a comedy intended

> as a sketch of country (Shropshire) manners as well as of the humours of the recruiting system. From both points of view the attempt was legitimate and novel, and attaches a certain historical interest to the picture in which it resulted. But the colours are in this comedy laid on as coarsely as in the lowest scenes of our eighteenth-century novels; there is little to choose between Captain Plume and Sergeant Kite, and hardly more between the young ladies and the country wenches of Shropshire.

In 1904 D. Schmid's *George Farquhar sein Leben und seine original Dramen* stressed the location of Farquhar's plays in the provinces. Charles Whilley's descriptive criticism in the *Cambridge History of English Literature* has not dated unduly, unlike that of J. E. Palmer, whose *The Comedy of Manners* (1913) presented Farquhar as failing to match his personal convictions and the current artistic and moral conventions, and carrying "the luscious treatment of sex" further than had other dramatists. G. H. Nettleton, however, in *English Drama of the Restoration and Eighteenth Century* (1914) praised him for presenting a whole gallery of full-length portraits, and for imparting individuality to his characters. E. Bernbaum gave a merely adequate account of his work in *The Drama of Sensibility* (1915). Louis A. Strauss in his Introduction to *A Discourse upon Comedy, The Recruiting Officer* and *The Beaux Stratagem* (1914) made penetrating remarks about Farquhar's characterisation. He regarded the tone of *The Recruiting Officer* as "anything but vicious; careless it certainly is". The play's "firmest moral ground", he argued, came from Silvia's unflagging devotion to Plume and his frank admiration of her sterling qualities, which he declares manly rather than womanish:

> Farquhar is at heart neither Cavalier nor Puritan, neither rake nor ascetic. He entered joyously into the game the former were playing without insight into its meaning or care as to its consequences. Troubled by the obviously just reproaches of the latter, he reacted upon this stimulus with little appreciation of its value. He was neither Cavalier nor Puritan, but a happy-go-lucky Celt who entered the world of waning conventions without prejudice as to forms of discipline, but with a mighty propensity for free living and the enjoyment of life.

William Archer in *The Old Drama and the New* (1923) differed "at almost every point" from Sir Adolphus Ward in his estimate of Farquhar:

> The critic [i.e. Ward] says: "While his [Farquhar's] morality is no better than that of the most reckless of his contemporaries, he has a coarseness of fibre which renders him less endurable than some of these are to a refined taste." I have tried to show that his morality is distinctly above the Restoration level and grows progressively better through his brief career. As to his being less "endurable" than his contemporaries, I can only say my experience is exactly the reverse. Farquhar gives me far more pleasure than any other playwright of his time. His coarseness is (to my thinking) much less nauseous than that of Wycherley and Congreve and he is a better dramatist and better writer than Cibber or Steele. He obviously and admittedly brought a breath of fresh air into comedy by taking it into the country, away from the purlieus of St. James's and Covent Garden; and even when he remained in town, he moved in a wholesome and genial climate as compared with the black, bitter and cruel atmosphere that weighs upon the works of his predecessors.

Archer took up Ward's comparison: he found in *The Recruiting*

Officer despite ethical standards which "cannot, certainly, be called high" a general tone of humanity:

> Captain Plume, though a loose-living soldier belongs rather to the company of Tom Jones than to that of Wycherley's Horner or Manly, Congreve's Bellmour or Vainlove, Vanburgh's Loveless or Worthy.

He praised Farquhar's ability to keep the action moving but disliked his "rather wanton use" of the aside, and thought that he "had not the skill to handle a complex intrigue plausibly".

In 1924 three critics wrote well on Farquhar. Allardyce Nicoll's *A History of English Drama* (1924; rev. ed. 1952) described *The Recruiting Officer* as a brilliantly successful comedy, which recaptured "a little of that Restoration spirit which the eighteenth-century authors seemed to be losing". Professor Nicoll traced the alteration in spirit from the politer drama of Congreve:

> There is, too, to be noted, the great realism of this comedy, in marked contradistinction to the element of artificiality traceable in the best plays of the preceding half century. The immorality, which before had been often graceful and debonair, has here developed into a coarse licentiousness, and that callousness which will be as marked as a characteristic of eighteenth century dramatic act is to be seen only too clearly in the abandonment of poor Rose, who, because of the reality of the play, seizes upon our sympathies. Even though she disappears amid the rioting of drunken laughter, we cannot forget her in her night of tears.

Joseph Wood Krutch in *Comedy and Conscience after the Restoration* (1924) stressed Farquhar's adherence to realism and satire rather than morality and sentiment while Bonamy Dobrée in *Restoration Comedy* (1924) gave us one of the sanest accounts of Farquhar's sense of humour.

There are useful comments on Farquhar's dramatic ability in H. Ten Eyck Perry's *The Comic Spirit in Restoration Drama* (1925) and Kathleen M. Lynch's *The Social Mode of Restoration Comedy* (1926). Peter Kavanagh's *The Irish Theatre* (1946) gave an account of the plays, and the author regarded Farquhar as a typical Irishman, stressing his dislike of fops and university men, and compared him to Shaw, pointing out his modernity, his preference for Shakespeare and Fletcher rather than Plautus and Menander. He considered the fortune-telling episode founded on Wilson's *The Cheats* and thought Plume a repetition of the character of Sir Harry Wildair, while Brazen and Worthy reflected the influence of Ben Jonson. Kite owed not a little to Falstaff and Master Shallow.

J. H. Smith's study, *The Gay Couple in Restoration Comedy* (1948), distinguished between two types of couples who think of courtship as a game.

> One is descended from that early form of the love game in which the heroine must take steps to cope with the hero's wildness: in the last decade of the century this function of hers had been expanded, and she may now be labelled the "pursuing heroine".

Silvia and Mrs Conquest in Cibber's *The Lady's Last Stake* are the best pursuing heroines and the "breeches" role (as distinguished from that of the veil in Spanish intrigue) is an English contribution. Worthy and Melinda are types of another kind of sex antagonism:

> After 1700 the conquest of a "difficult" lady most frequently amounts to little more than her purely captious "No" and the victory which the gallant (as likely as not a mere fortune hunter) wins over this resistance by taking whatever advantage his nimble wits suggest.

In this study the point is made that benevolence is a quality of the man and woman of sense (the doctrine that a love of one's fellow is natural to mankind is found first in Farquhar's *Love and a Bottle*), and it is further argued that Farquhar had some inkling of Hobbes's view of human nature and the opposing view.

Willard Connely's lively, sympathetic, and definitive life, *Young George Farquhar, the Restoration Drama at Twilight* (1949) contains a good summary of *The Recruiting Officer* and relates the play to its setting and to Farquhar's own recruiting tour. Y. H. Fujimara, *The Restoration Comedy of Wit* (1952) deals with the "Ledonic" principle in Farquhar's work, and Frederick S. Boas gave a good general account of Farquhar in *An Introduction to 18th Century Drama 1700–1780* (1953). Bonamy Dobrée's all too brief account in *English Literature in the Early Eighteenth Century* (1959) (Vol. VII of *The Oxford History of English Literature*) is to the point. He regards Farquhar as bringing to English society that cool, appraising glance, that sense of the falsity of assumptions, that mocking critical spirit, which is so often the gift of the Irishman. He is, in a sense, the Shaw of his time.

Eric Rothstein, in his *George Farquhar* (1967) has written a good chapter on *The Recruiting Officer*, endeavouring successfully to theorise on the reasons why Farquhar's conventional characters, his use of a situation perfectly familiar to himself and probably to his audience, and his militaristic attitude moved his play away from his earlier harsh moral melodrama into a new kind of comedy.

III Stage History

The Recruiting Officer was first performed at the Theatre Royal, Drury Lane, on Monday, 8 April 1706. (The cast is listed on p. 26). This was an extremely successful performance, and the play was repeated on 9, 10, 12, 13, 15, 17 and 20 April. It was also played on 11 and 20 June and a Gala Performance was given at Bath on 16 September. In the autumn of 1706, however, when the "war" between the theatres began[1] Rich put it on at Dorset Gardens (after Swiney had taken over most of his company to play at the Queen's Theatre, Haymarket), on 24 October to open his new season. He repeated it on Friday, 1 November. It was played at the Queen's Theatre on Thursday, 14 November (with Keen playing Ballance, Mills Worthy, Wilks Plume, Pack Kite, Bullock Bullock, Norris Pearmain, Fairbank Appletree, Mrs Oldfield Silvia and Mrs Bignal Rose), on Monday 18 November (with Mrs Porter as Melinda) and on Saturday, 30 November. That same Saturday it was also played in Drury Lane, with Eastcourt as "the true Serjeant Kite", a role he repeated in the same theatre on

[1] Emmett Avery has written a good account of this, describing how in the 1706–7 season "theatrical competition was altered by an agreement between John Vanbrugh and Owen Swiney permitting the latter to manage the Queen's, an arrangement which according to Cibber, Swiney undertook with the consent and possibly the collusion of Rich, the Manager of Drury Lane. Rich even permitted some of his principal actors—Cibber, Wilks, Johnson, Mills, Bullock, Mrs Oldfield—to go to the Queen's; and, as the roster of Rich's company shows, Rich had a very small number of actors in his employ in 1706–7. Although Cibber felt puzzled by Rich's motives, he eventually explained his former manager's actions by pointing to Rich's contempt for actors and his preference for singing, dancing and 'exotic entertainments'." See his *The London Stage 1660–1800, Part 2 1700–1729*, p. 129, and see also Colley Cibber's *Apology*, I, 330–36; II, 2–3.

Saturday, 7 December. The Queen's Theatre put it on again on Thursday, 19 December and Saturday, 28 December, with Fairbank as Kite, Kent as Appletree.

In 1707 *The Recruiting Officer* was played frequently (probably on 16 or 17 occasions) in both theatres. There was a new Prologue on 2 January, while Eastcourt's benefit was on 20 February in Drury Lane. In the same theatre on 17 March Penkethman spoke the Epilogue "riding on an Ass". Both theatres again played it simultaneously on 17 April.

A brief agreement was reached in January 1708 that Drury Lane should have the sole right to act plays while the Queen's had a monopoly of Italian opera. When the theatres became competitive again in the 1709–10 season, *The Recruiting Officer* was again staged in both theatres. On 24 February 1709 Wilks received £90 14*s.* 9*d.* for his benefit.

The play had become one of the best stock plays, with about a dozen performances in 1709. (There is some doubt about the performance on 6 September.) Eastcourt's benefit night, on 13 July 1710, provided an unusual episode, recorded by Emmett Avery:

> On this occasion the actors represented a prodigiously satirical Interscenium which was not to be found in the printed copy of the play. In this interlude a troop of soldiers came on, singing at the top of their voices an English song which had been made by the army in Flanders about the Duke of Marlborough. In it Prince Eugene is praised for his open-handedness, while Marlborough on the other hand, is blamed for his avarice, so that every verse ended: "but Marlborough not a penny." The people who are very bitter against the whole family, even the Duke himself, laughed prodigiously, and bandied about monstrous insults, although Marlborough's daughter, the Duchess of Montagu, was herself at the play and was so greatly shamed she was covered with blushes. . . . When the song was at an end, there was such a clapping and yelling that the actors were unable to proceed for nearly a quarter of an hour.

Eastcourt had another benefit, on 3 April 1711, and on this occasion the Epilogue showed "the Power of Beauty over a Soldier" in a song by Kite, "to a Tune just arriv'd from Ghent".

It has been calculated[1] that *The Recruiting Officer* was presented on

[1] See *The Recruiting Officer*, ed. Michael Shugrue, 1966, p. XX.

447 occasions between 1706 and 1776. Mention of particular performances must therefore be selective, since it never missed a season for seventy years after its first performance. Lacy Ryan played Plume effectively on many occasions, particularly at Lincoln's Inn Fields in 1730; the New Lincoln's Inn Fields Theatre opened with *The Recruiting Officer* in 1730, as had the theatre in Goodman's Fields two years previously. Peg Woffington played Silvia opposite Ryan when she first appeared at Covent Garden in 1740, and the younger Cibber played Brazen at the same time. David Garrick appeared in his first season as Costar Pearmain in 1742, and played Plume later the same year, at Drury Lane, with Charles Macklin as Brazen (his first stage appearance was at an amateur production of *The Recruiting Officer* in which he played Serjeant Kite at the age of eleven). A French version, *L'Officier en Recrue* was staged in London in the 1749–50 season. In 1756 Barry played Plume, in 1758 Palmer. The two captains were played by Smith and Woodward in 1763, by Crawford and King in 1781, and by Bannister the Younger and Dodd in 1791. Kemble played Plume in 1797 (Haymarket) and in 1812 and 1819 (Covent Garden). An interesting eighteenth-century production was that of 4 June 1789 which took place in a hut at Sydney, New South Wales. This was the first play performed in Australia and was acted by convicts.

The play was popular in the nineteenth century in provincial theatres, according to C. Stonehill, *The Complete Works of George Farquhar*, 1930, II, 39. In the twentieth century it has also been performed with success. Sir Nigel Playfair played Kite at the Haymarket in 1916 (an Incorporated Stage Society production), Trevor Howard played Plume in the Arts Theatre productions of 1943 and 1944, and in 1963 Sir Laurence Olivier played Brazen, Robert Stephens Plume, Colin Blakely Kite, Maggie Smith Silvia and Lynn Redgrave Rose. This was the fourth production of the National Theatre and it was directed by William Gaskill. It is illustrated copiously in the text edited by Kenneth Tynan in 1965.

A NOTE ON THE TEXT

The copy text used for this edition is the British Museum copy, 11773.g.11, of the first edition (1706). This has been collated with other copies of the first edition in the Bodleian Library, in the Victoria and Albert Museum, Forster Collection, F 4° 6976/22, and another in the Dyce and Forster Collection, F.D.11.14, in the National Library of Scotland, Edinburgh, in the Houghton Library, Harvard University, and in Yale University Library. No important press corrections are revealed by collation.

Corrections of the first edition made in "The Second Edition Corrected", published on 23 May 1706,[1] and "The Third Edition Corrected", published in the first week of December 1786,[2] have been recorded in the Textual Notes. Copies of the second, "corrected", edition in the British Museum, the Bodleian Library, Harvard University Library, and Yale University Library have been examined, as well as copies of the third, "corrected", edition in the Bodleian Library, Harvard University Library, Yale University Library, and the Library of Congress.

The text of the first edition has been closely followed in the present edition, as it was presumably set from Farquhar's MS. Thus some of its apparent errors may be attributed to his style, and, in some cases, to his desire to capture colloquial and rustic usages, rather than to the work of a careless compositor.

The first edition was printed "for Bernard Lintott at the Cross Keys next Nando's Coffee House near Temple Bar". It has been recorded that Lintott paid Farquhar £16 2*s.* 6*d.* for the manuscript from which the first quarto was presumably set.[3] The play was published on 12

[1] *The Daily Courant*, 23 May 1706.

[2] *The Daily Courant*, 28 November 1706, announced that it would be published on 3 December; it was advertised in *The Daily Courant*, 6 December 1706, and was probably published on that day.

[3] "Lintott's Accounts", *Literary Anecdotes of the Eighteenth Century*, ed. John Nichols (London, 1814) VIII, 296.

April 1706,[1] four days after the first highly successful production at the Theatre Royal, Drury Lane.[2]

The second, "corrected", edition contained substantive revisions (which are listed in the Textual Notes of the present edition). These alterations correct careless setting in the first edition; they also alter and regularise Farquhar's idiosyncratic grammar and syntax as well as his versions of rustic and colloquial speech. There are also alterations which refine the speech and the general tone of the play, probably because of the pressure of the Lord Chamberlain against any play containing "Profane or Indecent Expressions". The Master of the Revels, Charles Killigrew, was, as a result of this pressure for more respectability in the theatres, reluctant to license anything "lewd and impious". The alterations recorded in the textual notes show how the play was changed to avoid giving offence. For instance, in the second edition Plume's song and a suggestive speech of Rose's in III i and all of V i are omitted. There is some expansion of II i, and ten lines in French in IV i are suppressed in favour of twenty in English.

The fourth edition was probably published in December 1707 or early in 1708. While the third and fourth editions follow the revisions of the second (as do *The Comedies of Mr. George Farquhar* [1708] and [1710?] and *The Works of the late Ingenious Mr. George Farquhar: Containing all his Letters, Poems, Essays and Comedies Published in his Lifetime* [1711]), the third edition is the last edition which might have received any attention from the author. Other editions are listed in the Bibliography.

In the present edition long s has been transcribed in accordance with modern usage throughout the text and the use of large and small capitals and italics has been made consistent. Significant changes made in the text are listed in the textual notes. The spelling of proper names has been regularised.

Both pointed brackets and square brackets in this edition are editorial. The former enclose material supplied by the editor; the latter have been used merely to distinguish between text and original stage directions where there is any danger of confusion, i.e. where a direction occurs in running text and not either ranged to the side or set on a

[1] *The Daily Courant*, 12 April 1706.

[2] See Emmett L. Avery, *The London Stage 1660–1800, Part Two: 1700–1729*, (Carbondale, Illinois, 1960) I, 122–23.

line by itself. The original square bracket of the copy text, which preceded every stage direction ranged to the right, has been abolished. Where directions such as "aside" occur set to the right in the copy text, they have been moved so that they now precede the sentence of speech to which they refer, thus clarifying the action.

THE

Recruiting Officer

A

COMEDY

As it is Acted at the

THEATRE ROYAL

IN

DRURY-LANE,

By Her MAJESTY's Servants.

Written by Mr. Farquhar.

— Captique dolis, donisque coacti.
Virg. Lib. II. Æneid.

LONDON:

Printed for BERNARD LINTOTT at the *Cross Keys* next
Nando's Coffee-House near *Temple-Bar*.

Price 1s 6d

TO

All Friends round

THE

Wrekin.

My Lords and Gentlemen,

Instead of the mercenary Expectations that attend Addresses of this nature, I humbly beg, that this may be received as an Acknowledgment for the Favours you have already confer'd; I have transgress'd the Rules of Dedication in offering you any thing in that style, without first asking your leave: But the Entertainment I found in *Shropshire* commands me to be grateful, and that's all I intend.

'Twas my good fortune to be order'd some time ago into the Place which is made the Scene of this Comedy; I was a perfect Stranger to every thing in *Salop*; but its Character of Loyalty, the Number of its Inhabitants, the Alacrity of the Gentlemen in recruiting the Army, with their generous and hospitable Reception of Strangers.

This Character I found so amply verify'd in every Particular, that you made Recruiting, which is the greatest Fatigue upon Earth to others, to be the greatest Pleasure in the World to me.

The Kingdom cannot shew better Bodies of Men, better Inclinations for the Service, more Generosity, more good Understanding, nor more Politeness than is to be found at the Foot of the *Wrekin*.

Some little Turns of Humour that I met with almost within the Shade of that famous Hill, gave the rise to this Comedy; and People were apprehensive, that, by the Example of some others, I would make the Town merry at the expence of the Country Gentlemen: But they forgot that I was to write a Comedy, not a Libel; and that whilst I held to Nature, no Person of any Character in your Country could suffer by being expos'd. I have drawn the Justice and the Clown in their *puris Naturalibus*; the one an apprehensive, sturdy, brave Blockhead; and the other a worthy, honest, generous Gentleman, hearty in his Country's Cause, and of as good an Understanding as I could give him, which I must confess is far short of his own.

I humbly beg leave to interline a Word or two of the Adventures of the *Recruiting Officer* upon the Stage. Mr. *Rich*, who commands the Company for which those Recruits were rais'd, has desir'd me to acquit him before the World of a Charge which he thinks lyes heavy upon him for acting this Play on Mr. *Durfey*'s Third Night.

Be it known unto all Men by these Presents, that it was my Act and Deed, or rather Mr. *Durfey*'s; for he *wou'd* play his Third Night against the First of mine. He brought down a huge Flight of frightful Birds upon me, when (Heaven knows) I had not a Feather'd Fowl in my Play, except one single *Kite*: But I presently made *Plume* a Bird, because of his Name, and *Brazen* another, because of the Feather in his Hat; and with these three I engag'd his whole Empire, which I think was as great a *Wonder* as any *in the Sun*.

But to answer his Complaints more gravely, the Season was far advanc'd; the Officers that made the greatest Figures in my Play were all commanded to their Posts abroad, and waited only for a Wind, which might possibly turn in less time than a Day: And I know none of Mr. *Durfey*'s Birds that had Posts abroad but his *Woodcocks*, and their Season is over; so that he might put off a Day with less Prejudice than the Recruiting Officer cou'd, who has this farther to say for himself, that he was posted before the other spoke, and could not with Credit recede from his Station.

These and some other Rubs this Comedy met with before it appear'd. But on the other hand, it had powerful Helps to set it forward: The Duke of *Ormond* encourag'd the Author, and the Earl of *Orrery* approv'd the Play—My *Recruits* were *reviewed* by my *General* and my *Collonel*, and could not fail to *pass Muster*; and still to add to my Success, they were rais'd among my *Friends round the Wrekin*.

This Health has the advantage over our other celebrated Toasts, never to grow worse for the wearing: 'Tis a lasting Beauty, old without Age, and common without Scandal. That you may live long to set it cheerfully round, and to enjoy the abundant Pleasures of your fair and plentiful Country, is the hearty wish of,

My Lords and Gentlemen,

Your most Obliged,

and most Obedient Servant,

Geo. Farquhar.

PROLOGUE

In Antient Times, when Hellen's fatal Charms
Rous'd the contending Universe to Arms,
The Graecian *Council happily deputes*
The Sly Ulysses *forth——to raise Recruits.*
The Artful Captain found, without delay,
Where Great Achilles, *a Deserter, lay.*
Him Fate had warn'd to shun the Trojan *Blows*:
Him Greece *requir'd——against their* Trojan *Foes.*
All the Recruiting Arts were needful here
To raise this Great, this tim'rous Volunteer.
Ulysses *well could talk——He stirs, he warns*
The warlike Youth——He listens to the Charms
Of Plunder, fine Lac'd Coats, and glitt'ring Arms.
Ulysses *caught the Young Aspiring Boy,*
And listed him who wrought the Fate of Troy.
Thus by Recruiting was bold Hector *slain:*
Recruiting thus Fair Hellen *did regain.*
It for One Hellen *such prodigious things*
Were acted, that they ev'n listed Kings;
If for one Hellen's *artful vicious Charms*
Half the transported World was found in Arms;
What for so Many Hellens *may We dare,*
Whose Minds, *as well as Faces, are so* Fair?
If, by One Hellen's *Eyes, Old* Greece *cou'd find*
It's Homer *fir'd to write——Ev'n* Homer *Blind;*
The Britains *sure beyond compare may write,*
That view so many Hellens *every Night.*

DRAMATIS PERSONAE

MEN		BY
Mr. *Ballance*, Mr. *Scale*, Mr. *Scruple*,	Three Justices,	Mr. *Keen*. Mr. *Phillips*. Mr. *Kent*.
Mr. *Worthy*,	a Gentleman of *Shropshire*,	Mr. *Williams*.
Captain *Plume*, Captain *Brazen*	Two Recruiting Officers,	Mr. *Wilks*. Mr. *Cibber*.
Kite,	Serjeant to *Plume*,	Mr. *Estcourt*.
Bullock,	a Countrey Clown,	Mr. *Bullock*.
Costar Pear-main, *Tho. Apple-Tree*,	Two Recruits,	Mr. *Norris*. Mr. *Fairbank*.

WOMEN		BY
Melinda,	a Lady of Fortune,	Mrs. *Rogers*.
Silvia,	Daughter to *Ballance*, in Love with *Plume*,	Mrs. *Oldfield*.
Lucy,	*Melinda*'s Maid,	Mrs. *Sapsford*.
Rose,	a Countrey Wench,	Mrs. *Mountfort*

Constable, Recruits, Mob, Servants and Attendants.

SCENE *SHREWSBURY*

ACT I

SCENE I

SCENE, *the Market-Place——Drum beats the Granadeer-March*

Enter Serjeant KITE, *follow'd by the Mob.*

KITE. *Making a Speech.* If any Gentlemen Soldiers, or others, have a mind to serve her Majesty, and pull down the *French* King, if any Prentices have severe Masters, any Children have undutiful Parents; if any Servants have too little Wages, or any Husband too much Wife, let them repair to the Noble Serjeant *Kite*, at the Sign of the *Raven*, in this good Town of *Shrewsbury*, and they shall receive present Relief and Entertainment.——

Gentlemen, I don't beat my Drums here to insnare or inveigle any Man; for you must know, Gentlemen, that I am a Man of Honour: Besides, I don't beat up for common Soldiers; no, I list only Granadeers, Granadeers, Gentlemen——Pray Gentlemen observe this Cap——This is the Cap of Honour, it dubs a Man a Gentleman in the drawing of a Tricker; and he that has the good Fortune to be born six Foot high, was born to be a Great Man——Sir, ⟨(*To one of the Mob.*)⟩ Will you give me leave to try this Cap upon your Head?

MOB. Is there no harm in't? Won't the Cap list me?

KITE. No, no, no more than I can,——Come, let me see how it becomes you.

MOB. Are you sure there be no Conjuration in it, no Gunpowder-plot upon me?

KITE. ——No, no, Friend; don't fear, Man.

MOB. My mind misgives me plaguely——Let me see it—— ⟨(*Going to put it on.*)⟩ It smells woundily of Sweat and Brimstone; pray, Serjeant, what Writing is this upon the Face of it?

KITE. *The Crown, or the Bed of Honour.*

MOB. Pray now, what may be that same *Bed of Honour*?

KITE. O, a mighty large Bed, bigger by half than the great Bed of

Ware, ten thousand People may lie in't together, and never feel one another.

MOB. My Wife and I wou'd do well to lie in't, for we don't care for feeling one another——But do Folk sleep sound in this same *Bed of Honour?*

KITE. Sound! Ay, so sound that they never wake.

MOB. Wauns! I wish again that my Wife lay there.

KITE. Say you so? Then I find Brother——

MOB. Brother! Hold there Friend, I'm no Kindred to you that I know of, as yet——Lookye Serjeant, no coaxing, no wheedling d'ye'see; if I have a mind to list, why so——If not, why 'tis not so——Therefore take your Cap and your Brothership back again, for I an't dispos'd at this present Writing——No coaxing, no Brothering me, Faith.

KITE. I coax! I wheedle! I'm above it. Sir, I have serv'd twenty Campaigns——But, Sir, you talk well, and I must own that you are a Man every Inch of you, a pretty young sprightly Fellow——I love a Fellow with a Spirit, but I scorn to coax, 'tis base; tho' I must say, that never in my Life have I seen a better built Man: How firm and strong he treads, he steps like a Castle! But I scorn to wheedle any Man——Come, honest Lad, will you take share of a Pot?

MOB. Nay, for that matter, I'll spend my Penny with the best he that wears a Head, that is, begging your Pardon Sir, and in a fair way.

KITE. Give me your hand then, and now Gentlemen, I have no more to say but this——Here's a Purse of Gold, and there is a Tub of humming Ale at my Quarters, 'tis the Queen's Money, and the Queen's Drink; She's a generous Queen, and loves her Subjects——I hope, Gentlemen, you won't refuse the Queen's Health.

ALL MOB. No, no, no.

KITE. Huzza then, huzza for the Queen, and the Honour of *Shropshire.*

ALL MOB. Huzza.

KITE. Beat Drum——

Exeunt, Drum beating the Granadeer-March

Enter PLUME *in a Riding Habit.*

PLUME. By the Granadeer-March that shou'd be my Drum, and by that Shout it shou'd beat with Success——Let me see——⟨*Looks on his Watch.*⟩ Four a Clock——at ten Yesterday Morning I left *London*——A hundred and twenty Miles in thirty Hours, is pretty smart riding, but nothing to the Fatigue of Recruiting.

Enter KITE.

KITE. Welcome to *Shrewsbury*, noble Captain, from the Banks of the *Danube* to the *Severn* side, noble Captain you are welcome.

PLUME. A very elegant Reception indeed, Mr. *Kite*, I find you are fairly enter'd into your Recruiting Strain——Pray what Success?

KITE. I have been here but a Week, and I have recruited five.

PLUME. Five! Pray, What are they?

KITE. I have listed the strong Man of *Kent*, the King of the Gypsies, a *Scotch* Pedlar, a Scoundrel Attorney, and a *Welsh* Parson.

PLUME. An Attorney! Wer't thou mad? List a Lawyer! Discharge him, discharge him this Minute.

KITE. Why Sir?

PLUME. Because I will have no Body in my Company that can write; a Fellow that can write, can draw Petitions——I say, this Minute discharge him.

KITE. And what shall I do with the Parson?

PLUME. Can he write?

KITE. Umh——He plays rarely upon the Fiddle.

PLUME. Keep him by all means——But how stands the Country affected? Were the People pleas'd with the News of my coming to Town?

KITE. Sir, the Mob are so pleas'd with your Honour, and the Justices and better sort of People are so delighted with me, that we shall soon do our Business——But, Sir, you have got a Recruit here that you little think of.

PLUME. Who?

KITE. One that you beat up for last time you were in the Country; you remember your old Friend *Molly* at the *Castle*.

PLUME. She's not with Child, I hope.

KITE. No, no, Sir;——She was brought to Bed Yesterday.

PLUME. *Kite*, you must Father the Child.

KITE. Humph——And so her Friends will oblige me to marry the Mother.

PLUME. If they shou'd, we'll take her with us, she can wash you know, and make a Bed upon occasion.

KITE. Ay, or unmake it upon Occasion, but your Honour knows that I'm marry'd already.

PLUME. To how many?

KITE. I can't tell readily——I have set them down here upon the back of the Muster-Roll. ((*Draws out the Muster-Roll.*)) Let me see——*Imprimis*, Mrs. *Sheely Snickereyes*, she sells Potatoes upon *Ormond-Key* in Dublin——*Peggy Guzzle*, the Brandy Woman at the Horse-Guard at *Whitehall*——*Dolly Waggon*, the Carrier's Daughter in *Hull*——Madamoseille *Van-Bottomflat* at the *Buss*——Then *Jenny Okam* the Ship-Carpenter's Widow at *Portsmouth*; but I don't reckon upon her, for she was marry'd at the same time to two Lieutenants of Marines, and a Man of War's Boatswain.

PLUME. A full Company, you have nam'd five——Come, make 'em half a Dozen, *Kite*——Is the Child a Boy or a Girl?

KITE. A Chopping Boy.

PLUME. Then set the Mother down in your List, and the Boy in mine; enter him a Granadeer by the Name of *Francis Kite*, absent upon *Furlow*——I'll allow you a Man's Pay for his Subsistence, and now go comfort the Wench in the Straw.

KITE. I shall, Sir.

PLUME. But hold, have you made any Use of your *German* Doctor's Habit since you arriv'd?

KITE. Yes, yes, Sir; and my Fame's all about the Country, for the most famous Fortune-teller that ever told a Lye; I was oblig'd to let my Landlord into the Secret for the Convenience of keeping it so; but he's an honest Fellow, and will be trusty to any Roguery that is confided to him: This Device, Sir, will get you Men, and me Money, which I think is all we want at present——But yonder comes your Friend, Mr. *Worthy*——Has your Honour any farther Commands?

PLUME. None at present. ((*Exit Kite.*)) 'Tis indeed the Picture of *Worthy*, but the Life's departed.

Enter WORTHY.

PLUME. What! Arms a-cross, *Worthy*! Methinks you shou'd hold 'em open when a Friend's so near——The Man has got the Vapours in his Ears I believe. I must expel this melancholy Spirit.

Spleen, thou worst of Fiends below,
Fly, I conjure thee by this Magick Blow.

Slaps WORTHY *on the Shoulder.*

WORTHY. *Plume!* My dear Captain, welcome, safe and sound return'd!

PLUME. I 'scap'd safe from *Germany*, and sound I hope from *London*, you see I have lost neither Leg, Arm, nor Nose—— Then for my inside, 'tis neither troubled with Sympathies nor Antipathies, and I have an excellent Stomach for roast beef.

WORTHY. Thou art a happy Fellow, once I was so.

PLUME. What ails thee, Man? No Inundations nor Earthquakes in *Wales*, I hope? Has your Father rose from the dead, and reassum'd his Estate?

WORTHY. No.

PLUME. Then, you are marry'd surely.

WORTHY. No.

PLUME. Then you are mad, or turning Quaker.

WORTHY. Come, I must out with it——Your once gay roving Friend is dwindled into an obsequious, thoughtful, romantick, constant Coxcomb.

PLUME. And pray, What is all this for?

WORTHY. For a Woman.

PLUME. Shake hands Brother, if you go to that——Behold me as obsequious, as thoughtful, and as constant a Coxcomb as your Worship.

WORTHY. For whom?

PLUME. For a Regiment——But for a Woman, 'sdeath, I have been constant to fifteen at a time, but never melancholy for one; and can the Love of one bring you into this Pickle? Pray, who is this miraculous *Hellen*?

WORTHY. A *Hellen* indeed, not to be won under a ten Years' Siege, as great a Beauty, and as great a Jilt.

PLUME. A Jilt! Pho——Is she as great a Whore?

WORTHY. No, no.

PLUME. 'Tis ten thousand pities——But who is she? Do I know her?

WORTHY. Very well.

PLUME. Impossible——I know no Woman that will hold out a ten Year's Siege.

WORTHY. What think you of *Melinda*?

PLUME. *Melinda!* Why she began to capitulate this time Twelve-month, and offer'd to surrender upon honourable Terms; and I advis'd you to propose a Settlement of five hundred Pound a Year to her, before I went last abroad.

WORTHY. I did, and she hearken'd to't, desiring only one Week to consider; when, beyond her Hopes, the Town was reliev'd, and I forc'd to turn my Siege into a Blockade.

PLUME. Explain, explain.

WORTHY. My Lady *Richly* her Aunt in *Flintshire* dies, and leaves her at this critical time twenty thousand Pound.

PLUME. Oh the Devil, what a delicate Woman was there spoil'd! But by the Rules of War now, *Worthy*, your Blockade was foolish——After such a Convoy of Provisions was enter'd the Place, you cou'd have no thought of reducing it by Famine——You shou'd have redoubled your Attacks, taken the Town by Storm, or have dy'd upon the Breach.

WORTHY. I did make one general Assault, and push'd it with all my Forces; but I was so vigorously repuls'd, that despairing of ever gaining her for a Mistress, I have alter'd my Conduct, given my Addresses the obsequious and distant turn, and court her now for a Wife.

PLUME. So, as you grew obsequious, she grew haughty, and because you approach'd her as a Goddess, she us'd you like a Dog.

WORTHY. Exactly.

PLUME. 'Tis the way of 'em all——Come *Worthy*, your obsequious and distant Airs will never bring you together; you must not think to surmount her Pride by your Humility——Wou'd you bring her to better Thoughts of you, she must be reduc'd to a meaner Opinion of her self——Let me see——The very first thing that I wou'd do, shou'd be to lie with her Chamber-maid, and hire three or four Wenches in the Neighbourhood to report that I had got them with Child. Suppose we lampoon'd all the pretty Women in Town, and left her out? Or what if we made a Ball, and forgot to invite her, with one or two of the Ugliest.

WORTHY. These wou'd be Mortifications, I must confess,—— But we live in such a precise, dull place, that we can have no Balls, no Lampoons, no——

PLUME. What! No Bastards! And so many Recruiting Officers in Town; I thought 'twas a Maxim among them to leave as many Recruits in the Country as they carry'd out.

WORTHY. No body doubts your Good-will, Noble Captain, in serving your Country with your best Blood——Witness our Friend *Molly* at the *Castle*——There have been Tears in Town about that Business, Captain.

PLUME. I hope *Silvia* has not heard of't.

WORTHY. O Sir, have you thought of her? I began to fancy you had forgot poor *Silvia*.

PLUME. Your Affairs had put my own quite out of my Head: 'Tis true, *Silvia* and I had once agreed to go to Bed together, cou'd we have adjusted Preliminaries; but she wou'd have the Wedding before Consummation, and I was for Consummation before the Wedding——We cou'd not agree, she was a pert obstinate Fool, and wou'd lose her Maiden-head her own way, so she may keep it for *Plume*.

WORTHY. But do you intend to marry upon no other Conditions.

PLUME. Your Pardon, Sir, I'll marry upon no Conditions at all, if I shou'd, I'm resolv'd never to bind my self to a Woman for my whole Life, till I know whether I shall like her Company for half an Hour——Suppose I marry'd a Woman that wanted a Leg? Such a thing might be, unless I examin'd the Goods before-hand; if People wou'd but try one another's Constitutions before they engag'd, it wou'd prevent all these Elopements, Divorces, and the Devil knows what.

WORTHY. Nay, for that matter, the Town did not stick to say, That——

PLUME. I hate Country Towns for that Reason——If your Town has a dishonourable Thought of *Silvia*, it deserves to be burnt to the Ground——I love *Silvia*, I admire her frank, generous Disposition; there's something in that Girl more than

Woman, her Sex is but a foil to her——The Ingratitude, Dissimulation, Envy, Pride, Avarice, and Vanity of her Sister Females, do but set off their Contraries in her——In short, were I once a General, I wou'd marry her.

WORTHY. Faith you have reason; for were you but a Corporal, she wou'd marry you——But my *Melinda* coquets it with every Fellow she sees——I lay fifty Pound she makes love to you.

PLUME. I'll lay fifty Pound that I return it, if she does——Lookye, *Worthy*, I'll win her, and give her to you afterwards.

WORTHY. If you win her, you shall wear her, Faith; I wou'd not give a Fig for the Conquest, without the Credit of the Victory.

Enter KITE.

KITE. Captain, Captain, a word in your Ear.

PLUME. You may speak out, here are none but Friends.

KITE. You know, Sir, that you sent me to comfort the good Woman in the Straw, Mrs. *Molly*——My Wife, Mr. *Worthy*.

WORTHY. Oho, very well——I wish you Joy, Mr. *Kite*.

KITE. Your Worship very well may,——for I have got both a Wife and a Child in half an Hour,——but as I was a saying, you sent me to comfort Mrs. *Molly*——My Wife, I mean. But what d'ye think Sir? She was better comforted before I came.

PLUME. As how?

KITE. Why, Sir, a Footman in a blue Livery had brought her ten Guineas to buy her Baby Cloaths.

PLUME. Who, in the Name of Wonder, cou'd send them?

KITE. Nay, Sir, I must whisper that——Mrs. *Silvia*.

((*Whispers*)) PLUME.

PLUME. *Silvia!* Generous Creature.

WORTHY. *Silvia!* Impossible.

KITE. Here be the Guinea's, Sir; I took the Gold as part of my Wife's Portion: Nay farther, Sir, she sent word that the Child shou'd be taken all imaginable Care of, and that she intended to stand God-mother. The same Footman, as I was coming to you with this News, call'd after me, and told me that his Lady wou'd speak with me——I went; and upon hearing that you were come to Town, she gave me half a Guinea for the News, and order'd me to tell you, That Justice *Balance* her Father, who is just come out of the Country, wou'd be glad to see you.

PLUME. There's a Girl for you, *Worthy*——Is there any thing of Woman in this? No, 'tis noble and generous, Manly Friendship, show me another Woman that wou'd lose an Inch of her Prerogative that way, without Tears, Fits, and Reproaches. The common Jealousie of her Sex, which is nothing but their Avarice of Pleasure, she despises; and can part with the Lover, tho' she dies for the Man——Come *Worthy*——Where's the best Wine? For there I'll quarter.

WORTHY. *Horton* has a fresh Pipe of choice *Barcelona*, which I wou'd not let him pierce before, because I reserv'd the Maidenhead of it for your welcome to Town.

PLUME. Let's away then——Mr. *Kite*, wait on the Lady with my humble Service, and tell her, That I shall only refresh a little, and wait on her.

WORTHY. Hold, *Kite*——Have you seen the other Recruiting Captain?

KITE. No, Sir.

PLUME. Another, who is he?

WORTHY. My Rival in the first place, and the most unaccountable Fellow——But I'll tell you more as we go.

Exeunt.

SCENE II

SCENE, *An Apartment*

MELINDA *and* SILVIA *Meeting.*

MELINDA. Welcome to Town, Cosin *Silvia* ((*Salute.*)) I envy'd you your Retreat in the Country; for *Shrewsbury*, methinks, and all your Heads of Shires, are the most irregular Places for living, here we have Smoak, Noise, Scandal, Affectation, and Pretension; in short, every thing to give the Spleen, and nothing to divert it——Then the Air is intolerable.

SILVIA. Oh! Madam, I have heard the Town commended for its Air.

MELINDA. But you don't consider, *Silvia*, how long I have liv'd in it; for I can assure you, that to a Lady the least nice in her

Constitution, no Air can be good above half a Year; Change of Air I take to be the most agreeable of any Variety in Life.

SILVIA. As you say, Cosin *Melinda*, there are several sorts of Airs, Airs in Conversation, Airs in Behaviour, Airs in Dress; then we have our Quality Airs, our sickly Airs, our reserv'd Airs, and sometimes our impudent Airs.

MELINDA. Pshaw——I talk only of the Air we breath, or more properly of that we taste——Have you not, *Silvia*, found a vast Difference in the Taste of Airs?

SILVIA. Pray Cosin, are not Vapours a sort of Air? Taste Air! You may as well tell me I might feed upon Air; but prithee, my dear *Melinda*, don't put on such Airs to me, your Education and mine were just the same, and I remember the time when we never troubled our Heads about Air, but when the sharp Air from the *Welsh* Mountains made our Noses drop in a cold Morning at the Boarding-School.

MELINDA. Our Education, Cosin, was the same, but our Temperaments had nothing alike; you have the Constitution of a Horse——

SILVIA. So far as to be troubled with neither Spleen, Cholick, nor Vapours, I need no Salt for my Stomach, no Hart's-horn for my Head, nor Wash for my Complexion; I can gallop all the Morning after the Hunting Horn, and all the Evening after a Fiddle: In short, I can do every thing with my Father but drink and shoot flying; and I'm sure I can do every thing my Mother cou'd, were I put to the Tryal.

MELINDA. You're in a fair way of being put to't; for I'm told, your Captain is come to Town.

SILVIA. Ay, *Melinda*, he is come, and I'll take care he shan't go without a Companion.

MELINDA. You're certainly mad, Cosin.

SILVIA. *And there's a Pleasure sure, in being mad,*
Which none but Mad-men know.

MELINDA. Thou poor Romantick *Quixote*, hast thou the Vanity to imagine that a young sprightly Officer that rambles over half the Globe in half a Year, can confine his Thoughts to the little Daughter of a Country Justice in an obscure corner of the World?

SILVIA. Pshaw! What care I for his Thoughts? I shou'd not like a Man with confin'd Thoughts, it shows a Narrowness of Soul.

Constancy is but a dull, sleepy Quality at best; they will hardly admit it among the Manly Vertues, nor do I think it deserves a Place with Bravery, Knowledge, Policy, Justice, and some other Qualities that are proper to that noble Sex. In short, *Melinda*, I think a Petticoat a mighty simple thing, and I'm heatily tir'd of my Sex.

MELINDA. That is, you are tir'd of an Appendix to our Sex, that you can't so handsomly get rid of in Petticoats as if you were in Breeches——O'my Conscience, *Silvia*, hadst thou been a Man, thou hadst been the greatest Rake in *Christendom*.

SILVIA. I shou'd endeavour to know the World, which a Man can never do thoroughly without half a hundred Friendships, and as many Amours. But now I think on't, how stands your Affair with Mr. *Worthy*?

MELINDA. He's my Aversion.

SILVIA. Vapours.

MELINDA. What do you say, Madam?

SILVIA. I say, that you shou'd not use that honest Fellow so inhumanely, he's a Gentleman of Parts and Fortune, and beside that he's my *Plume*'s Friend; and by all that's sacred, if you don't use him better, I shall expect Satisfaction.

MELINDA. Satisfaction! You begin to fancy your self in Breeches in good earnest——But to be plain with you, I like *Worthy* the worse for being so intimate with your Captain; for I take him to be a loose, idle, unmannerly Coxcomb.

SILVIA. Oh! Madam——You never saw him, perhaps, since you were Mistress of twenty thousand Pound; you only knew him when you were capitulating with *Worthy* for a Settlement, which perhaps might incourage him to be a little loose and unmannerly with you.

MELINDA. What do you mean, Madam?

SILVIA. My meaning needs no Interpretation, Madam.

MELINDA. Better it had, Madam——for methinks you're too plain.

SILVIA. If you mean the Plainness of my Person, I think your Ladyship as plain as me to the full.

MELINDA. Were I assur'd of that, I shou'd be glad to take up with a Rakely Officer as you do.

SILVIA. Again! Look'e, Madam——You're in your own House.

MELINDA. And if you had kept in yours, I shou'd have excus'd you.

SILVIA. Don't be troubl'd, Madam——I shan't desire to have my visit return'd.

MELINDA. The sooner therefore you make an end of this, the better.

SILVIA. I'm easily advis'd to follow my Inclinations——So Madam——Your humble Servant.

Exit.

MELINDA. Saucy thing!

Enter LUCY.

LUCY. What's the matter, Madam?

MELINDA. Did you not see the proud Nothing, how she swells upon the Arrival of her Fellow?

LUCY. Her Fellow has not been long enough arriv'd to occasion any great swelling, Madam——I don't believe she has seen him yet.

MELINDA. Nor shan't if I can help it; let me see——I have it ——Bring me Pen and Ink——Hold, I'll go write in my Closet.

LUCY. An Answer to this Letter, I hope, Madam——((*Presents a letter.*))

MELINDA. Who sent it?

LUCY. Your Captain, Madam——

MELINDA. He's a Fool, and I'm tir'd of him; send it back unopen'd.

LUCY. The Messenger's gone, Madam——

MELINDA. Then how shall I send an Answer? call him back immediately, while I go write.

Exeunt severally.

ACT II

SCENE I

An Apartment

Enter Justice BALLANCE *and* PLUME.

BALLANCE. Look'e, Captain, give us but Blood for our Money, and you shan't want Men; I remember, that for some Years of the last War, we had no Blood nor Wounds but in the Officers Mouths, nothing for our Millions but News Papers not worth a reading, our Armies did nothing but play at Prison Bars, and hide and seek with the Enemy, but now ye have brought us Colours, and Standards, and Prisoners; odsmylife, Captain, get us but another Mareschal of *France*, and I'll go my self for a Soldier.

PLUME. Pray, Mr. *Ballance*, how does your fair Daughter?

BALLANCE. Ah! Captain, what is my Daughter to a Mareschal of *France*? We're upon a nobler Subject, I want to have a particular Description of the Battel of *Hochstet*.

PLUME. The Battel, Sir, was a very pretty Battel as one shou'd desire to see, but we were all so intent upon Victory, that we never minded the Battel; all that I know of the matter is, our General commanded us to beat the *French*, and we did so, and if he pleases to say the word, we'll do't again——But pray, Sir, how does Mrs. *Silvia*?

BALLANCE. Still upon *Silvia*! For shame, Captain——You're engag'd already, wedded to the War, Victory is your Mistress, and it is below a Soldier to think of any other.

PLUME. As a Mistress, I confess, but as a Friend, Mr. *Ballance*.

BALLANCE. Come, come, Captain, never mince the matter, wou'd not you debauch my Daughter if you cou'd?

PLUME. How Sir! I hope she is not to be debauch'd.

BALLANCE. Faith but she is, Sir, and any Woman in *England* of her Age and Complexion, by a Man of your Youth and Vigour. Look'e, Captain, once I was young, and once an Officer as you are; and I can guess at your Thoughts now by what mine were then, and I remember very well, that I wou'd have given one of my Legs to have deluded the Daughter of an old plain Country Gentleman, as like me as I was then like you.

PLUME. But, Sir, was that Country Gentleman your Friend and Benefactor?

BALLANCE. Not much of that.

PLUME. There the Comparison breaks; the Favours, Sir, that——

BALLANCE. Pho! I hate Speeches; if I have done you any Service, Captain, 'twas to please my self, for I love thee; and if I cou'd part with my Girl, you shou'd have her as soon as any young

Fellow I know; but I hope you have more Honour than to quit the Service, and she more Prudence than to follow the Camp: But she's at her own Disposal, she has fifteen hundred Pound in her Pocket, and so, *Silvia, Silvia.* ⟨*Calls.*⟩

Enter SILVIA.

SILVIA. There are some Letters, Sir, come by the Post from *London*, I left them upon the Table in your Closet.

BALLANCE. And here is a Gentleman from *Germany.* ⟨*Presents* PLUME *to her.*⟩ Captain, you'll excuse me, I'll go read my Letters and wait on you.

Exit

SILVIA. Sir, you're welcome to *England.*

PLUME. Blessings in Heaven we shou'd receive in a prostrate Posture, let me receive my welcome thus. ⟨*Kneels and kisses her Hand.*⟩

SILVIA. Pray rise, Sir, I'll give you fair Quarter.

PLUME. All Quarter I despise, the Height of Conquest is to die at your Feet. ⟨*Kissing her Hand again.*⟩

SILVIA. Well, well, you shall die at my Feet, or where you will; but first let me desire you to make your Will, perhaps you'll leave me something.

PLUME. My Will, Madam, is made already, and there it is, ⟨*Gives her a Parchment*⟩ and if you please to open that Parchment, which was drawn the Evening before the Battel of *Blenheim*, you will find whom I left my Heir. ⟨SILVIA *opens the Will, and reads.*⟩

SILVIA. Mrs. *Silvia Ballance*——Well, Captain, this is a handsome and a substantial Compliment, but I can assure you I am much better pleas'd with the bare knowledge of your Intention, than I shou'd have been in the Possession of your Legacy; but methinks, Sir, you shou'd have left something to your little Boy at the *Castle.*

PLUME. That's home; ⟨*Aside*⟩ my little Boy! Lack-a-day, Madam, that alone may convince you 'twas none of mine; why the Girl, Madam, is my Serjeant's Wife, and so the poor Creature gave out that I was Father, in hopes that my Friends might support her in case of Necessity, that was all Madam,——my Boy! No, no.

Enter Servant.

SERVANT. Madam, my Master has receiv'd some ill News from *London*, and desires to speak with you immediately, and he begs the Captain's Pardon that he can't wait on him as he promis'd.

PLUME. Ill News! Heavens avert it; nothing cou'd touch me nearer than to see that generous worthy Gentleman afflicted; I'll leave you to comfort him, and be assur'd that if my Life and Fortune can be any way serviceable to the Father of my *Silvia*, he shall freely command both.

SILVIA. The Necessity must be very pressing, that wou'd engage me to do either.

Exeunt severally.

SCENE II

SCENE, *changes to another Apartment*

Enter BALLANCE *and* SILVIA.

SILVIA. Whilst there is Life there is hope, Sir; perhaps my Brother may recover.

BALLANCE. We have but little reason to expect it. Dr. *Kilman* acquaints me here, that before this comes to my hands, he fears I shall have no Son——Poor *Owen*! But the Decree is just, I was pleas'd with the Death of my Father, because he left me an Estate, and now I'm punish'd with the Loss of an Heir to inherit mine. I must now look upon you as the only Hopes of my Family, and I expect that the Augmentation of your Fortune will give you fresh Thoughts and new Prospects.

SILVIA. My desire of being punctual in my Obedience, requires that you wou'd be plain in your Commands, Sir.

BALLANCE. The Death of your Brother makes you sole Heiress to my Estate, which three or four Years hence will amount to twelve hundred Pound *per Annum*; this Fortune gives you a fair Claim to Quality and a Title, you must set a just Value upon your self, and in plain Terms think no more of Captain *Plume*.

SILVIA. You have often commended the Gentleman, Sir.

BALLANCE. And I do so still, he's a very pretty Fellow; but tho' I lik'd him well enough for a bare Son-in-Law, I don't approve of him for an Heir to my Estate and Family, fifteen hundred Pound, indeed, I might trust in his hands, and it might do the young Fellow a Kindness, but odsmylife, twelve hundred Pound a Year wou'd ruine him, quite turn his Brain. A Captain of Foot worth twelve hundred Pound a Year! 'Tis a Prodigy in Nature: Besides this, I have five or six thousand Pounds in Woods upon my Estate; Oh! That wou'd make him stark mad, for you must know that all Captains have a mighty Aversion to Timber, they can't endure to see Trees standing; then I shou'd have some Rogue of a Builder by the help of his damn'd Magick Art transform my noble Oaks and Elms into Cornishes, Portals, Sashes, Birds, Beasts, Gods and Devils, to adorn some magotty, new-fashion'd Bauble upon the *Thames*; and then you shou'd have a Dog of a Gardner bring a *Habeas Corpus* for my *Terra Firma*, remove it to *Chelsea* or *Twitnam*, and clap it into Grass-plats and Gravel-walks.

Enter a Servant.

SERVANT. Sir, here's one below with a Letter for your Worship, but he will deliver it into no hands but your own.

BALLANCE. Come, show me the Messenger.

Exit with Servant.

SILVIA. Make the Dispute between Love and Duty, and I am Prince *Prettyman* exactly——If my Brother dies, Ah! poor Brother; if he lives, Ah! poor Sister——'Tis bad both ways, I'll try again, follow my own Inclinations and break my Father's Heart, or obey his Commands and break my own, worse and worse——Suppose I take thus——A moderate Fortune, a pretty Fellow and a Pad,——or a fine Estate, a Coach and six, and an Ass——That will never do neither.

Enter BALLANCE *and Servant.*

BALLANCE. ⟨*To the Servant who goes out.*⟩ Put four Horses into the Coach. *Silvia.*

SILVIA. Sir.

BALLANCE. How old were you when your Mother dy'd?

SILVIA. So young that I don't remember I ever had one; and you have been so careful, so indulgent to me since, that indeed I never wanted one.

Ballance. Have I ever deny'd you any thing you ask'd of me?

Silvia. Never, that I remember.

Ballance. Then *Silvia*, I must beg that once in your Life you wou'd grant me a Favour.

Silvia. Why shou'd you question it, Sir?

Ballance. I don't, but I wou'd rather counsel than command——I don't propose this with the Authority of a Parent, but as the Advice of your Friend, that you wou'd take the Coach this Moment, and go into the Country.

Silvia. Does this Advice proceed from the Contents of the Letter you receiv'd just now?

Ballance. No matter, I shall be with you in three or four days, and then give you my Reasons——But before you go, I expect you will make me one solemn Promise.

Silvia. Propose the thing, Sir.

Ballance. That you will never dispose of your self to any Man, without my Consent.

Silvia. I promise.

Ballance. Very well, and to be even with you, I promise, That I will never dispose of you without your own Consent; and so *Silvia*, the Coach is ready, farewel. ⟨*Leads her to the Door and returns.*⟩ Now she's gone, I'll examine the Contents of this Letter a little nearer. ⟨*Reads.*⟩

Sir,

My Intimacy with Mr. Worthy *has drawn a Secret from him, that he had from his Friend Captain* Plume, *and my Friendship and Relation to your Family oblige me to give you timely notice of it; the Captain has dishonourable Designs upon my Cosin* Silvia. *Evils of this Nature are more easily prevented than amended, and that you wou'd immediately send my Cosin into the Country is the Advice of,*

Sir, Your humble Servant,
Melinda.

Why the Devil's in the young Fellows of this Age, they're ten times worse than they were in my time; had he made my Daughter a Whore, and forswore it like a Gentleman, I cou'd have almost pardon'd it; but to tell Tales before-hand is monstrous! Hang it, I can fetch down a Woodcock or Snipe, and why not a Hat and Feather? I have a Case of good Pistols, and have a good mind to try.

Enter WORTHY.

BALLANCE. *Worthy*, your Servant.

WORTHY. I'm sorry, Sir, to be the Messenger of ill News.

BALLANCE. I apprehend it, Sir; you have heard that my Son *Owen* is past Recovery.

WORTHY. My Advices say he's dead, Sir.

BALLANCE. He's happy, and I am satisfy'd; the Strokes of Heaven I can bear, but Injuries from Men, Mr. *Worthy*, are not so easily supported.

WORTHY. I hope, Sir, you are under no Apprehension of Wrong from any Body?

BALLANCE. You know I ought to be.

WORTHY. You wrong my Honour, Sir, in believing I cou'd know any thing to your Prejudice without resenting it as much as you shou'd.

BALLANCE. This Letter, Sir, which I tear in pieces to conceal the Person that sent it, informs me that *Plume* has a Design upon *Silvia*, and that you are privy to't.

WORTHY. Nay, then Sir, I must do my self Justice, and endeavour to find out the Author. ⟨*Takes up a piece of the Letter.*⟩ Sir, I know the Hand, and if you refuse to discover the Contents, *Melinda* shall tell me. ⟨*Going.*⟩

BALLANCE. Hold, Sir, the Contents I have told you already, only with this Circumstance, that her Intimacy with Mr. *Worthy* had drawn the Secret from him.

WORTHY. Her Intimacy with me!——Dear Sir, let me pick up the pieces of this Letter, 'twill give me such a hank upon her Pride, to have her own an Intimacy under her hand, 'twas the luckiest Accident. ⟨*Gathering up the Letter.*⟩ The Aspersion, Sir, was nothing but Malice, the Effect of a little Quarrel between her and Mrs. *Silvia*.

BALLANCE. Are you sure of that, Sir?

WORTHY. Her Maid gave me the History of part of the Battel just now, as she overheard it.

BALLANCE. 'Tis probable, I am satisfy'd.

WORTHY. But I hope, Sir, your Daughter has suffer'd nothing upon the Account?

BALLANCE. No, no——Poor Girl, she is so afflicted with the News of her Brother's Death, that to avoid Company she beg'd Leave to be gone into the Country.

WORTHY. And is she gone?

BALLANCE. I cou'd not refuse her, she was so pressing, the Coach went from the door the Minute before you came——

WORTHY. So pressing to be gone, Sir——I find her Fortune will give her the same Airs with *Melinda*, and then *Plume* and I may laugh at one another.

BALLANCE. Like enough——Women are as subject to Pride as we are, and why mayn't great Women as well as great Men forget their old Acquaintance——But come——Where's this young Fellow, I love him so well, it wou'd break the Heart of me to think him a Rascal ⟨*Aside.*⟩ I'm glad my Daughter's gone fairly off tho'. Where does the Captain quarter?

WORTHY. At *Horton*'s, I'm to meet him there two Hours hence, and we shou'd be glad of your Company.

BALLANCE. Your pardon, dare *Worthy*, I must allow a Day or two to the Death of my Son; the Decorum of Mourning is what we owe the World, because they pay it to us afterwards. I'm yours over a Bottle, or how you will.

WORTHY. Sir, I'm your humble Servant.

Exeunt severally.

SCENE III

SCENE, *the Street*

Enter KITE, *with one of the Mob in each hand, drunk.*

KITE *sings.*

Our Prentice TOM *may now refuse*
To wipe his scoundrel Master's Shoes;
For now he's free to sing and play,
Over the Hills and far away——Over the Hills, &c.

The Mob sing the Chorus.

We all shall lead more happy Lives,
By getting rid of Brats and Wives,
That scold and brawl both Night and Day;
Over the Hills and far away——*Over the Hills, &c.*

KITE. Hey Boys——Thus we Soldiers live, drink, sing, dance, play; we live, as one shou'd say——We live——'Tis impossible to tell how we live——We're all Princes——Why——Why you're a King——You're an Emperour, and I'm a Prince——Now——an't we——

1st MOB. No, Serjeant——I'll be no Emperour.

KITE. No!

1st MOB. No, I'll be a Justice of Peace.

KITE. A Justice of Peace, Man!

1st MOB. Ay, wauns will I, for since this pressing Act they are greater than any Emperor under the Sun.

KITE. Done, you're a Justice of Peace, and you're a King, and I'm a Duke, and a Rum Duke, an't I?

2d MOB. No, but I'll be no King.

KITE. What then?

2d MOB. I'll be a Queen.

KITE. A Queen!

2d MOB. Ay, Queen of *England*——That's greater than any King of 'em all.

KITE. Bravely said! Faith! Huzza for the Queen. ⟨*All Huzza.*⟩ But heark'e, you Mr. Justice, and you Mr. Queen, did you ever see the Queen's Picture?

1st AND 2d MOB. No, no.

KITE. I wonder at that, I have two of 'em set in Gold, and as like her Majesty, God bless the Mark. ⟨*He takes two Broad Pieces out of his Pocket.*⟩ See here, they're set in Gold. ⟨*Gives one to each.*⟩

1st MOB. ⟨*Looking earnestly upon the Piece.*⟩ The wonderful Works of Nature!

2d MOB. What's this written about? Here's a Posy, I believe, *Ca-ro-lus*——What's that Serjeant?

KITE. O *Carolus*——Why *Carolus* is Latin for Queen *Ann,* that's all.

2d MOB. 'Tis a fine thing to be a Scollard, Serjeant, will you part with this? I'll buy it on you, if it come within the Compass of a Crown.

KITE. A Crown! Never talk of buying——'Tis the same thing among Friends you know, I present them to you both, you shall give me as good a thing; put them up, and remember your old Friend, when I'm *over the Hills and far away.* ⟨*Singing.*⟩
They sing and put up the Money.

Enter PLUME *singing.*

Over the Hills, and o'er the Main,
To Flanders, Portugal, *or Spain;*
The Queen commands, and we'll obey,
Over the Hill and far away.

Come on my Men of Mirth, away with it, I'll make one among ye; who are these hearty Lads?

KITE. Off with your Hats, Ouns, off with your Hats; this is the Captain, the Captain.

1st MOB. We have seen Captains afore now, mun.

2d MOB. Ay, and Lieutenant Captains too; Flesh, I'se keep on my Nab.

1st MOB. And I'se scarcely d'off mine for any Captain in *England*, my Vether's a Freeholder.

PLUME. Who are these jolly Lads, Serjeant?

KITE. A couple of honest brave Fellows, that are willing to serve the Queen; I have entertain'd them just now as Volunteers under your Honour's Command.

PLUME. And good Entertainment they shall have, Volunteers are the Men I want, those are the Men fit to make Soldiers, Captains, Generals.

1st MOB. Wauns, *Tummas*, What's this? Are you listed?

2d MOB. Flesh, not I, are you, *Costar*?

1st MOB. Wauns, not I.

KITE. What, not listed! Ha, ha, ha, a very good Jest, Faith.

1st MOB. Come, *Tummas*, we'll go whome.

2d MOB. Ay, ay, come.

KITE. Home! For shame, gentlemen, behave yourselves better before your Captain——Dear *Tummas*, honest *Costar*——

2d MOB. No, no, we'll be gone. ⟨*Going.*⟩

KITE. Nay, then I command you to stay, I place you both Centinels in this place for two Hours to watch the Motion of St. *Mary*'s Clock you, and you the Motion of St. *Chads*, and he that dare stir from his Post till he be relieved, shall have my Sword in his Guts the next Minute.

PLUME. What's the matter, Serjeant——I'm afraid you're too rough with these Gentlemen.

KITE. I'm too mild, Sir, they disobey Command, Sir, and one of them shou'd be shot for an Example to the other.

1st MOB. Shot! *Tummas.*

PLUME. Come, Gentlemen, what is the matter?

1st MOB. We don't know, the noble Serjeant is pleas'd to be in a Passion, Sir——But

KITE. They disobey Command, they deny their being listed.

2d MOB. Nay, Serjeant, we don't downright deny it neither, that we dare not do for fear of being shot; but we humbly conceive in a civil way, and begging your Worship's Pardon that we may go home.

PLUME. That's easily known, have either of you receiv'd any of the Queen's Money?

1st MOB. Not a brass Farthing, Sir.

KITE. Sir, they have each of them receiv'd three and twenty Shillings and Six-pence, and 'tis now in their Pockets.

1st MOB. Wauns! If I have a Penny in my Pocket, but a bent Six-pence, I'll be content to be listed, and shot into the Bargain.

2d MOB. And I, look'e here, Sir.

1st MOB. Ay, here's my Stock too, nothing but the Queen's Picture that the Serjeant gave me just now.

KITE. See there, a broad Piece, three and twenty Shillings and Six-pence, the t'other has the Fellow on't.

PLUME. The Case is plain, Gentlemen, the Goods are found upon you, those Pieces of Gold are worth three and twenty and Six-pence each.

1st MOB. So it seems that *Carolus* is three and twenty Shillings and Six-pence in Latin.

2d MOB. 'Tis the same thing in the *Greek*, for we are listed.

1st MOB. Flesh, but we an't *Tummas*, I desire to be carry'd before the Mayar, Captain. 〈*While they talk, the Captain and Serjeant whisper.*〉

PLUME. 'Twill never do, *Kite*; your damn'd Tricks will ruine me at last, I won't lose the Fellows tho', if I can help it——Well,

Gentlemen, there must be some Trick in this, my Serjeant offers here to take his Oath that you're fairly listed.

1st MOB. Why, Captain, we know that you Soldiers have more Liberty of Conscience than other Folks, but for me or Neighbour *Costar* here to take such an Oath, 'twou'd be downright Perjuration.

PLUME. Look'e, you Rascal, you Villain, if I find that you have impos'd upon these two honest Fellows, I'll trample you to Death, you Dog; come, how was't?

2d MOB. Nay, then we will speak, your Serjeant, as you say, is a Rogue, begging your Worship's Pardon——And——

1st MOB. Nay, *Tummas*, let me speak, you know I can read; and so, Sir, he gave us those two pieces of Money for Pictures of the Queen by way of a Present.

PLUME. How! By way of a Present! The Son of a Whore! I'll teach him to abuse honest Fellows like you; Scoundrel, Rogue, Villain, &c. ⟨*Beats the Serjeant off the Stage, and follows him out.*⟩

BOTH MOB. O brave Noble Captain, huzza, a brave Captain, Faith.

1st MOB. Now *Tummas, Corolus* is Latin for a beating: This is the bravest Captain I ever saw, Wauns, I have a Month's mind to go with him.

Re-enter PLUME.

PLUME. A Dog! To abuse two such pretty Fellows as you; Look'e, Gentlemen, I love a pretty Fellow, I come among you here as an Officer to list Soldiers, not as a Kidnapper, to steal Slaves.

1st MOB. Mind that, *Tummas*.

PLUME. I desire no Man to go with me, but as I went my self, I went a Volunteer, as you or you may go, for a little time carry'd a Musket, and now I command a Company.

2d MOB. Mind that, *Costar*, a sweet Gentleman.

PLUME. 'Tis true, Gentlemen, I might take an advantage of you, the Queen's Money was in your Pockets; my Serjeant was ready to take his Oath that you were listed, but I scorn to do a base thing, you are both of you at your Liberty.

1st MOB. Thank you, Noble Captain, I cod, I cannot find in my Heart to leave him, he talks so finely.

2d Mob. Ay, *Coster*, wou'd he alway hold in this Mind.

Plume. Come, my Lads, one thing more I'll tell you, you're both young tight Fellows, and the Army is the place to make you Men for ever, every Man has his Lot, and you have yours; What think you now of a Purse full of *French* Gold out of a Monsieur's Pocket, after you have dash'd out his Brains with the But of your Firelock, eh——

1st Mob. Wauns, I'll have it, Captain, give me a Shilling, I'll follow you to the end of the World.

2d Mob. Nay, dear *Costar*, duna, be advis'd.

Plume. Here, my Heroe, here are two Guineas for thee, as earnest of what I'll do farther for thee.

2d Mob. Duna take it, duna, dear *Costar*. ⟨*Cries and pulls back his Arm.*⟩

1st Mob. I wull, I wull, Wauns, my Mind gives me that I shall be a Captain my self; I take your Money, Sir, and now I'm a Gentleman.

Plume. Give me thy hand——And now you and I will travel the World o're, and command wherever we tread—— ⟨*Aside*⟩. Bring your Friend with you if you can.

1st Mob. Well, *Tummas*, must we part——

2d Mob. No, *Costar*, I cannot leave thee——Come, Captain. ⟨*Crying.*⟩ I'll e'ne go along too; and if you have too honester, simpler Lads in your Company that we twa been——I'll say no more——

Plume. Here, my Lad ⟨*Gives him Money*⟩ now your Name.

1st Mob. *Thummas Appletree.*

Plume. And yours?

2d Mob. *Costar Pearmain.*

Plume. Born where?

1st Mob. Both in *Herefordshire.*

Plume. Very well; Courage, my Lads, now we will sing *Over the Hills and far away.*

Courage, Boys, 'tis one to ten,
But we return all Gentlemen, &c.

ACT III

SCENE I

The Market-Place

PLUME *and* WORTHY.

WORTHY. I can'nt forbear admiring the Equality of our two Fortunes, we lov'd two Ladies; they met us half way, and just as we were upon the point of leaping into their Arms, Fortune drops into their Laps, Pride possesses their Hearts, a Maggot fills their Heads, Madness takes 'em by the Tails, they snort, kick up their Heels, and away they run.

PLUME. And leave us here to mourn upon the Shore——a couple of poor melancholy Monsters——What shall we do?

WORTHY. I have a Trick for mine; the Letter you know, and the Fortune-teller.

PLUME. And I have a Trick for mine.

WORTHY. What is't?

PLUME. I'll never think of her again.

WORTHY. No!

PLUME. No; I think my self above administring to the Pride of any Woman, were she worth twelve thousand a Year, and I han't the Vanity to believe I shall ever gain a Lady worth twelve hundred; the generous good-natur'd *Silvia* in her Smock I admire, but the haughty scornful *Silvia*, with her Fortune, I despise.

A SONG.

I

Come, fair one, be kind
You never shall find
A Fellow so fit for a Lover:
The World shall view
My Passion for you,
But never your Passion discover.

2

I still will complain
Of your Frowns and Disdain,
Tho I revel thro' all your Charms:
The World shall declare,
That I die with Despair,
When I only die in your Arms.

3

I still will adore,
And love more and more,
But, by Jove, if you chance to prove cruel:
I'll get me a Miss
That freely will kiss,
Tho' I afterwards drink Water-gruel.

What! Sneak out o' Town, and not so much as a Word, a Line, a Complement! 'Sdeath, now far off does she live? I'll go and break her Windows.

WORTHY. Ha, ha, ha; ay, and the Window Bars too to come at her. Come, come, Friend, no more of your rough Military Airs.

Enter KITE.

KITE. Captain, Sir, look yonder, she's a coming this way, 'tis the prettiest cleanest little Tit——

PLUME. Now, *Worthy*, to show you how much I'm in Love ——Here she comes, and what is that great Country Fellow with her?

KITE. I can't tell, Sir.

Enter ROSE *and her Brother* BULLOCK, ROSE *with a Basket on her Arm, crying Chickens.*

ROSE. Buy Chickens, young and tender——young and tender Chickens.

PLUME. Here, you Chickens——

ROSE. Who calls?

PLUME. Come hither, pretty Maid.

ROSE. Will you please to buy, Sir?

WORTHY. Yes, Child, we'll both buy.

PLUME. Nay, *Worthy*, that's not fair, market for your self; come, my Child, I'll buy all you have.

ROSE. Then all I have is at your Sarvice. *Curtsies.*

WORTHY. Then I must shift for my self, I find. *Exit.*

PLUME. Let me see——Young and tender, you say? 〈*Chucks her under the Chin.*〉

ROSE. As ever you tasted in your Life, Sir. *Curtsies.*

PLUME. Come, I must examine your Basket to the Bottom, my Dear.

ROSE. Nay, for that matter, put in your hand, feel, Sir; I warrant my Ware as good as any in the Market.

PLUME. And I'll buy it all, Child, were it ten times more.

ROSE. Sir, I can furnish you.

PLUME. Come then; we won't quarrel about the Price, they're fine Birds; pray what's your Name, pretty Creature.

ROSE. *Rose*, Sir, my Father is a Farmer within three short Mile o' th' Town; we keep this Market, I sell Chickens, Eggs, and Butter, and my Brother *Bullock* there sells Corn.

BULLOCK. Come, Sister, hast ye, we shall be liate a whome. 〈*All this while* BULLOCK *whistles about the Stage.*〉

PLUME. *Kite*! 〈*He tips the wink upon* KITE, *who returns it.*〉 Pretty Mrs. *Rose*! You have——Let me see——How many?

ROSE. A Dozen, Sir——And they are richly worth a Crawn.

BULLOCK. Come *Ruose, Ruose*, I sold fifty Stracke o'Barley to Day in half this time; but you will higgle and higgle for a Penny more than the Commodity is worth.

ROSE. What's that to you, Oaf? I can make as much out of a Groat, as you can out of four-pence, I'm sure——The Gentleman bids fair, and when I meet with a Chapman, I know how to make the best on him——And so, Sir, I say, for a Crawn Piece the Bargain is yours.

PLUME. Here's a Guinea, my Dear.

ROSE. I con't change your Money, Sir.

PLUME. Indeed, indeed but you can——My Lodging is hard by, you shall bring home the Chickens, and we'll make Change there.

Goes off, she follows him.

KITE. So, Sir, as I was telling you, I have seen one of these *Hussars* eat up a Ravelin for his Breakfast, and afterwards pick his Teeth with a Palisado.

BULLOCK. Ay, you Soldiers see very strange things——But pray, Sir, what is a Ravelin?

KITE. Why 'tis like a modern minc'd Pye, but the Crust is confounded hard, and the Plumbs are somewhat hard of Digestion!

BULLOCK. Then your Palisado, pray what may he be?——Come, *Ruose*, pray ha' done.

KITE. Your Palisado is a pretty sort of Bodkin, about the Thickness of my Leg.

BULLOCK. 〈*Aside.*〉 That's a Fib, I believe——Eh, where's *Ruose*, *Ruose*, *Ruose*, 'sflesh, where's *Ruose* gone?

KITE. She's gone with the Captain.

BULLOCK. The Captain! Wauns, there's no pressing of Women, sure.

KITE. But there is, Sir.

BULLOCK. If the Captain shou'd press *Ruose*, I shou'd be ruin'd; which way went she——O! The Devil take your Rablins and Palisaders.

Exit.

KITE. You shall be better acquainted with them, honest *Bullock*, or I shall miss of my Aim.

Enter WORTHY.

WORTHY. Why, thou'rt the most useful Fellow in Nature to your Captain, admirable in your way, I find.

KITE. Yes, Sir, I understand my Business, I will say it; you must know, Sir, I was born a Gypsie, and bred among that Crew till I was ten Year old, there I learn'd Canting and Lying; I was bought from my Mother *Cleopatra* by a certain Nobleman for three Pistols, who liking my Beauty made me his Page, there I learn'd Impudence and Pimping; I was turn'd off for wearing my Lord's Linen, and drinking my Lady's Brandy, and then turn'd Bailiff's Follower, there I learn'd Bullying and Swearing——I at last got into the Army, and there I learn'd Whoring and Drinking——So that if your Worship pleases to cast up the whole Sum, *viz.* Canting, Lying, Impudence, Pimping, Bullying,

Swearing, Whoring, Drinking, and a Halbard, you will find the Sum Total will amount to a Recruiting Serjeant.

WORTHY. And pray, what induc'd you to turn Soldier?

KITE. Hunger and Ambition——The Fears of starving and Hopes of a Truncheon, led me along to a Gentleman with a fair Tongue and fair Perriwig, who loaded me with Promises; but I gad 'twas the lightest Load that I ever felt in my Life——He promis'd to advance me, and indeed he did so——To a Garret in the *Savoy*——I ask'd him why he put me in Prison, he call'd me lying Dog, and said I was in Garrison, and indeed 'tis a Garrison that may hold out till Doom's-day before I shou'd desire to take it again; but here comes Justice *Ballance*.

Enter BALLANCE *and* BULLOCK.

BALLANCE. Here, you Serjeant, where's your Captain? Here's a poor foolish Fellow comes clamouring to me with a Complaint, that your Captain has press'd his Sister, do you know anything of this Matter, *Worthy*?

WORTHY. Ha, ha, ha, I know his Sister is gone with *Plume* to his Lodgings to sell him some Chickens.

BALLANCE. Is that all? The Fellow's a Fool.

BULLOCK. I know that, an't please you; but if your Worship pleases to grant me a Warrant to bring her before you for fear o'th' worst.

BALLANCE. Thou art a mad Fellow, thy Sister's safe enough.

KITE. ⟨*Aside.*⟩ I hope so too.

WORTHY. Hast thou no more Sense, Fellow, than to believe that the Captain can list Women?

BULLOCK. I know not whether they list them, or what they do with them, but I'm sure they carry as many Women as Men with them out of the Country.

BALLANCE. But how came you not to go along with your Sister?

BULLOCK. Luord, Sir, I thought no more of her going than I do of the Day I shall die; but this Gentleman, here, not suspecting any Hurt neither, I believe——You thought no Harm, Friend, did ye?

KITE. Lack-a-day, Sir, not I—— ⟨*Aside.*⟩ Only that I believe I shall marry her to Morrow.

BALLANCE. I begin to smell Powder——Well, Friend, but what did that Gentleman with you?

BULLOCK. Why, Sir, he entertain'd me with a fine Story of a great Fight between the *Hungarians*, I think it was, and the *Irish*; and so, Sir, while we were in the heat of the Battel, the Captain carry'd off the Baggage.

BALLANCE. Serjeant, go along with this Fellow to your Captain, give him my humble Service, and I desire him to discharge the Wench, tho' he has listed her.

BULLOCK. Ay——And if he ben't free for that, he shall have another Man in her place.

KITE. Come, honest Friend—— ⟨*Aside.*⟩ You shall go to my Quarters instead of the Captain's.

Exeunt KITE *and* BULLOCK.

BALLANCE. We must get this mad Captain his Compliment of Men, and send him a packing, else he'll over-run the Country.

WORTHY. You see, Sir, how little he values your Daughter's Disdain.

BALLANCE. I like him the better, I was much such another Fellow at his Age; I never set my Heart upon any Woman so much as to make me uneasie at the Disappointment, but what was very surprising both to my self and Friends, I chang'd o'th' sudden from the most fickle Lover to the most constant Husband in the World; but how goes your affair with *Melinda*?

WORTHY. Very slowly, *Cupid* had formerly Wings, but I think in this Age he goes upon Crutches, or I fancy *Venus* has been dallying with her Cripple *Vulcan* when my Amour commenc'd, which has made it go on so lamely; my Mistress has got a Captain too, but such a Captain! As I live yonder he comes.

BALLANCE. Who? That bluff Fellow in the Sash. I don't know him.

WORTHY. But I engage he knows you, and every Body at first sight; his Impudence were a Prodigy, were not his Ignorance proportionable; he has the most universal Acquaintance of any Man living, for he won't be alone, and no body will keep him Company twice; then he's a *Cæsar* among the Women, *Veni, Vidi, Vici*, that's all. If he has but talk'd with the Maid, he swears he has lain with the Mistress; but the most surprizing part of his

Character is his Memory, which is the most prodigious, and the most trifling in the World.

BALLANCE. I have met with such Men, and I take this good-for-nothing Memory to proceed from a certain Contexture of the Brain, which is purely adapted to Impertinencies, and there they lodge secure, the Owner having no Thoughts of his own to disturb them. I have known a Man as perfect as a Chronologer as to the Day and Year of most important Transactions, but be altogether ignorant of the Causes, Springs, or Consequences of any one thing of moment; I have known another acquire so much by Travel, as to tell you the Names of most Places in *Europe*, with their Distances of Miles, Leagues or Hours, as punctually as a Post-boy; but for any thing else, as ignorant as the Horse that carries the Mail.

WORTHY. This is your Man, Sir, add but the Traveller's Privilege of lying, and even that he abuses; this is the Picture, behold the Life!

Enter BRAZEN.

BRAZEN. Mr. *Worthy*, I'm your Servant, and so forth—— Heark'e my Dear——

WORTHY. Whispering, Sir, before Company is not Manners, and when no body's by, 'tis foolish.

BRAZEN. Company! *Mor't de ma vie*, I beg the Gentleman's Pardon, who is he?

WORTHY. Ask him.

BRAZEN. So I will——My Dear, I'm your Servant, and so forth, your Name, my Dear?

BALLANCE. Very *Laconick*, Sir.

BRAZEN. *Laconick*, a very good Name truly; I have known several of the *Laconicks* abroad, poor *Jack Laconick*! He was kill'd at the Battel of *Landen*. I remember that he had a blew Ribbond in his Hat that very Day, and after he fell, we found a piece of Neat's Tongue in his Pocket.

BALLANCE. Pray Sir, did the *French* attack us, or we them, at *Landen*?

BRAZEN. The *French* attack us! Oons, Sir, are you a Jacobite?

BALLANCE. Why that Question?

BRAZEN. Because none but a Jacobite cou'd think that the *French* durst attack us——No, Sir, we attack'd them on the——I have reason to remember the time, for I had two and twenty Horses kill'd under me that Day.

WORTHY. Then, Sir, you rid mighty hard.

BALLANCE. Or perhaps, Sir, like my Countryman, you rid upon half a dozen Horses at once.

BRAZEN. What d'e mean, Gentlemen, I tell you they were kill'd; all torn to pieces by Cannon-shot, except six that I stak'd to Death upon the Enemies *Chevaux de Frise*.

BALLANCE. Noble Captain, may I crave your Name?

BRAZEN. *Brazen*, at your Service.

BALLANCE. Oh, *Brazen*! A very good Name, I have known several of the *Brazens* abroad.

WORTHY. Do you know Captain *Plume*, Sir?

BRAZEN. Is he any thing related to *Frank Plume* in *Northamptonshire*——Honest *Frank*! Many, many a dry Bottle have we crack'd hand to fist; you must have known his Brother *Charles* that was concern'd in the *India* Company, he marry'd the Daughter of Old *Tongue-Pad* the Master in Chancery, a very pretty Woman, only squinted a little; she dy'd in Child-bed of her first Child, but the Child surviv'd, 'twas a Daughter, but whether 'twas call'd *Margaret* or *Marjory*, upon my Soul, I can't remember——But, Gentlemen ⟨*Looking on his Watch*⟩. I must meet a Lady, a twenty thousand Pounder presently, upon the Walk by the Water——*Worthy*, your Servant, *Laconick*, yours.

Exit.

BALLANCE. If you can have so mean an Opinion of *Melinda*, as to be jealous of this Fellow, I think she ought to give you Cause to be so.

WORTHY. I don't think she encourages him so much for gaining her self a Lover, as to set me up a Rival; were there any Credit to be given to his words, I shou'd believe *Melinda* had made him this Assignation; I must go see——Sir, you'll pardon me.

BALLANCE. Ay, ay, Sir, you're a Man of Business; but what have we got here?

Enter ROSE *singing what she pleases.*

ROSE. And I shall be a Lady, a Captain's Lady; and ride single upon a white Horse with a Star, upon a Velvet Side-saddle, and I shall go to *London* and see the Tombs and the Lions, and the Queen. Sir——an't please your Worship, I have often seen your Worship ride thro' our Grounds a hunting, begging your Worship's Pardon——Pray what may this Lace be worth a Yard?

Showing some Lace.

BALLANCE. Right *Mechelin*, by this Light! Where did you get this Lace, Child?

ROSE. No matter for that, Sir, I come honestly by't.

BALLANCE. I question it much.

ROSE. And see here, Sir, a fine Turky-shell Snuff-box, and fine Mangeree, see here; ⟨*She takes Snuff affectedly*⟩ the Captain learnt me how to take it with an Air.

BALLANCE. Oho, the Captain! Now the Murder's out, and so the Captain taught you to take it with an Air?

ROSE. Yes, and give it with an Air, too——Will your Worship please to taste my Snuff. ⟨*Offers the Box affectedly.*⟩

BALLANCE. You'r a very apt Scholar, pretty Maid, and pray what did you give the Captain for these fine things?

ROSE. He's to have my Brother for a Soldier, and two or three Sweet-hearts that I have in the Country, they shall all go with the Captain; O he's the finest Man, and the humblest withal, wou'd you believe it, Sir? He carry'd me up with him to his own Chamber with as much Familiarity, as if I had been the best Lady in the Land.

BALLANCE. O he's a mighty familiar Gentleman as can be.

ROSE. But I must beg your Worship's Pardon, I must go seek out my Brother *Bullock*. *Runs off singing.*

BALLANCE. If all Officers took the same Method of Recruiting with this Gentleman, they might come in time to be Fathers as well as Captains of their Companies.

Enter PLUME *singing.*

PLUME. *But it is not so*
With those that go
Thro' Frost and Snow
Most apropo,
My Maid with the Milking-pail.

Takes hold on ROSE.

How, the Justice! Then I'm arraign'd, condemn'd, and executed.

BALLANCE. Oh, my Noble Captain.

ROSE. And my Noble Captain too, Sir.

PLUME. 'Sdeath, Child, are you mad?——Mr. *Ballance*, I am so full of Business about my Recruits, that I ha'n't a Moment's time to——I have just now three or four People to——

BALLANCE. Nay, Captain, I must speak to you.

ROSE. And so must I too, Captain.

PLUME. Any other time, Sir; I cannot for my Life, Sir——

BALLANCE. Pray, Sir.

PLUME. Twenty thousand things——I wou'd but——now, Sir, pray——Devil take me——I cannot——I must——⟨*Breaks away.*⟩

BALLANCE. Nay, I'll follow you.

Exit.

ROSE. And I too.

Exit.

SCENE II

SCENE, *the Walk, by the* SEVERN *side.*

Enter MELINDA *and her Maid* LUCY.

MELINDA. And pray, was it a Ring, or Buckle, or Pendants, or Knots; or in what Shape was the Almighty Gold transform'd that has brib'd you so much in his Favour?

LUCY. Indeed, Madam, the last Bribe I had was from the Captain, and that was only a small piece of *Flanders* edging for Pinners.

MELINDA. Ay, *Flanders* Lace is as constant a Present from Officers to their Women, as something else is from their Women to them. They every Year bring over a Cargo of Lace to cheat the Queen of her Duty, and her Subjects of their Honesty.

LUCY. They only barter one sort of prohibited Goods for another, Madam.

MELINDA. Has any of them been bartering with you, Mrs. Pert, that you talk so like a Trader?

LUCY. Madam, you talk as peevishly to me as if it were my Fault, the Crime is none of mine tho' I pretend to excuse it; tho' he shou'd not see you this Week can I help it? But as I was saying,

Madam, his Friend Captain *Plume* has so taken him up these two Days——

MELINDA. Psha! wou'd his Friend, the Captain, were ty'd on his Back; I warrant he has never been sober since that confounded Captain came to Town: The Devil take all Officers, I say, they do the Nation more harm by debauching us at home, than they do good by defending us abroad: No sooner a Captain comes to Town, but all the young Fellows flock about him, and we can't keep a Man to our selves.

LUCY. One wou'd imagine, Madam, by your Concern for *Worthy*'s Absence, that you shou'd use him better when he's with you.

MELINDA. Who told you, pray, that I was concern'd for his Absence? I'm only vex'd that I've had nothing said to me these two Days: One may like the Love, and despise the Lover, I hope; as one may love the Treason, and hate the Traytor. Oh! here comes another Captain, and a Rogue that has the Confidence to make Love to me; but indeed I don't wonder at that, when he has the Assurance to fancy himself a fine Gentleman.

LUCY. ⟨*Aside.*⟩ If he shou'd speak o'th' Assignation, I shou'd be ruin'd.

Enter BRAZEN.

BRAZEN. ⟨*Aside.*⟩ True to the Touch, Faith. I'll draw up all my Complements into one grand Platoon, and fire upon her at once.

Thou peerless Princess of Salopian *Plains,*
Envy'd by Nymphs, and worship'd by the Swains,
Behold how humbly do's the Severn *glide,*
To greet thee Princess of the Severn *side.*

Madam, I'm your humble Servant, and all that, Madam—— A fine River this same *Severn*, do you love Fishing, Madam?

MELINDA. 'Tis a pretty melancholy Amusement for Lovers.

BRAZEN. I'll go buy Hooks and Lines presently; for you must know, Madam, that I have serv'd in *Flanders* against the *French*, in *Hungary* against the *Turks*, and in *Tangier* against the *Moors*, and I was never so much in Love before; and split me, Madam, in all the Campaigns I ever made I have not seen so fine a Woman as your Ladyship.

MELINDA. And from all the Men I ever saw I never had so fine a Complement; but you Soldiers are the best bred Men, that we must allow.

BRAZEN. Some of us, Madam, but there are Brutes among us too, very sad Brutes; for my own part, I have always had the good Luck to prove agreeable: I have had very considerable Offers, Madam, I might have marry'd a *German* Princess worth Fifty thousand Crowns a Year, but her Stove disgusted me; the Daughter of a *Turkish Bashaw* fell in Love with me too when I was Prisoner among the Infidels, she offer'd to rob her Father of his Treasure, and make her Escape with me, but I don't know how, my time was not come, Hanging and Marriage, you know, go by Destiny; Fate has reserved me for a *Shropshire* Lady with twenty thousand Pound——Do you know any such Person, Madam?

MELINDA. Extravagant Coxcomb! to be sure a great many Ladies of that Fortune wou'd be proud of the Name of Mrs. *Brazen.*

BRAZEN. Nay, for that matter, Madam, there are Women of very good Quality of the Name of *Brazen.*

Enter WORTHY.

MELINDA. O! are you there, Gentleman?——Come, Captain, we'll walk this way, give me your Hand.

BRAZEN. My Hand, Heart's Blood and Guts are at your Service. ——Mr. *Worthy,*——your Servant, my Dear.

Exit leading MELINDA.

WORTHY. Death and Fire! this is not to be born.

Enter PLUME.

PLUME. No more it is, Faith.

WORTHY. What?

PLUME. The *March* Beer at the *Raven*; I have been doubly serving the Queen,——raising Men, and raising the Excise——Recruiting and Elections are good Friends to the Excise.

WORTHY. You an't drunk?

PLUME. No, no, whimsical only; I cou'd be mighty foolish, and fancy my self mighty witty; Reason still keeps its Throne, but it nods a little, that's all.

WORTHY. Then you're just fit for a Frolick?

PLUME. As fit as close Pinners for a Punk in the Pit.

WORTHY. There's your Play then, recover me that Vessel from that *Tangerine.*

PLUME. She's well rigg'd, but how is she mann'd?

WORTHY. By Captain *Brazen* that I told you of to Day; the Frigot is call'd the *Melinda*, a first Rate I can assure you; she sheer'd off with him just now on purpose to affront me, but according to your Advice I wou'd take no notice, because I wou'd seem to be above a Concern for her Behaviour; but have a care of a Quarrel.

PLUME. No, no, I never quarrel with any thing in my Cups but with an Oyster Wench or a Cook Maid, and if they ben't civil, I knock 'em down: But heark'e my Friend, I will make Love, and I must make Love,——I tell'e what, I'll make Love like a Platoon.

WORTHY. A Platoon! how's that?

PLUME. I'll kneel, stoop and stand, Faith; most Ladies are gain'd by Platooning.

WORTHY. Here they come; I must leave you.

Exit.

PLUME. Soh——Now I must look as sober and demure as a Whore at a Christning.

Enter BRAZEN *and* MELINDA.

BRAZEN. Who's that, Madam?

MELINDA. A Brother Officer of yours, I suppose.

BRAZEN. Ay!—— ⟨*To* PLUME.⟩ My Dear.

PLUME. My Dear! *They run and embrace.*

BRAZEN. My dear Boy, how is't?——Your Name, my Dear, if I be not mistaken, I have seen your Face.

PLUME. I never see your's in my Life, my Dear——But there's a Face well known as the Sun's, that shines on all, and is by all ador'd.

BRAZEN. Have you any Pretensions, Sir?

PLUME. Pretensions!

BRAZEN. That is, Sir, have you ever serv'd abroad?

PLUME. I have serv'd at Home, Sir; For Ages serv'd this cruel Fair——And that will serve the turn, Sir.

MELINDA. Soh——Between the Fool and the Rake, I shall bring

a fine spot of Work upon my hands——I see *Worthy* yonder, I cou'd be content to be Friends with him wou'd he come this way.

BRAZEN. Will you fight for the Lady, Sir?

PLUME. ⟨*Aside.*⟩ No, Sir, but I'll have her notwithstanding.

> *Thou Peerless Princess of* Salopian *Plains,*
> *Envy'd by Nymphs, and worshipp'd by the Swains.*

BRAZEN. Oons, Sir, not fight for her!

PLUME. Prithee be quiet, I shall be out.

> *Behold how humbly do's the* Severn *glide*
> *To greet thee, Princess of the* Severn *side.*

BRAZEN. Don't mind him, Madam, if he were not so well drest I shou'd take him for a Poet; but I'll show the Difference presently——Come, Madam, we'll place you between us, and now the longest Sword carries her. ⟨*Draws,* MELINDA *shrieks.*⟩

Enter WORTHY.

MELINDA. Oh! Mr. *Worthy*, save me from these Madmen.

Runs off with WORTHY.

PLUME. Ha, ha, ha, why don't you follow, Sir, and fight the bold Ravisher?

BRAZEN. No, Sir, you're my Man.

PLUME. I don't like the Wages, and I won't be your Man.

BRAZEN. Then you're not worth my Sword.

PLUME. No! Pray what did it cost?

BRAZEN. It cost my Enemies thousands of Lives, Sir.

PLUME. Then they had a dear Bargain.

Enter SILVIA *drest in Man's Apparel.*

SILVIA. Save ye, save ye, Gentlemen.

BRAZEN. My Dear, I'm yours.

PLUME. Do you know the Gentleman?

BRAZEN. No, but I will presently——Your Name, my Dear.

SILVIA. *Wilfull, Jack Wilfull*, at your Service.

BRAZEN. What! The *Kentish Wilfulls*, or those of *Staffordshire*?

SILVIA. Both Sir, both; I'm related to all the *Wilfulls* in *Europe*, and I'm Head of the Family at present.

PLUME. Do you live in the Country, Sir?

SILVIA. Yes, Sir, I live where I shou'd; I have neither Home, House, nor Habitation beyond this spot of Ground.

BRAZEN. What are you, Sir?

SILVIA. A Rake.

PLUME. In the Army I presume.

SILVIA. No, but I intend to list immediately——Look'e, Gentlemen, he that bids me fairest shall have me.

BRAZEN. Sir, I'll prefer you, I'll make you a Corporal this Minute.

PLUME. A Corporal! I'll make you my Companion, you shall eat with me.

BRAZEN. You shall drink with me.

PLUME. You shall lie with me, you young Rogue. 〈*Kisses her.*〉

BRAZEN. You shall receive your Pay, and do no Duty.

SILVIA. Then you must make me a Field-Officer.

PLUME. Pho, pho, I'll do more than all this, I'll make you a Corporal, and give you a Brevet for Serjeant.

BRAZEN. Can you read and write, Sir?

SILVIA. Yes.

BRAZEN. Then your Business is done, I'll make you Chaplain to the Regiment.

SILVIA. Your Promises are so equal, that I'm at a loss to chuse, there is one *Plume* that I hear much commended in Town, pray which of you is Captain *Plume*?

PLUME. I'm Captain *Plume*.

BRAZEN. No, no, I am Captain *Plume*.

SILVIA. Hey day!

PLUME. Captain *Plume*, I'm your Servant, my Dear.

BRAZEN. Captain *Brazen*, I'm yours——The Fellow dare not fight.

Enter KITE, *goes to whisper* PLUME.

KITE. Sir, if you please——

PLUME. No, no, there's your Captain——Captain *Plume*, your Serjeant here has got so drunk he mistakes me for you.

BRAZEN. He's an incorrigible Sot——Here, my Hector of *Holbourn*, forty Shillings for you.

PLUME. I forbid the Banes——Look'e, Friend, you shall list with Captain *Brazen*.

SILVIA. I will see Captain Brazen hang'd first, I will list with Captain *Plume*; I'm a free-born *Englishman*, and will be a Slave my own way—— ⟨*To* BRAZEN.⟩ Look'e, Sir, will you stand by me?

BRAZEN. I warrant you, my Lad.

SILVIA. Then I will tell you, Captain *Brazen* ⟨*To* PLUME⟩ that you are an ignorant, pretending, impudent Coxcomb.

BRAZEN. Ay, ay, a sad Dog.

SILVIA. A very sad Dog, give me the Money Noble Captain *Plume*.

PLUME. Hold, hold, then you won't list with Captain *Brazen*?

SILVIA. I won't.

BRAZEN. Never mind him, Child, I'll end the Dispute presently; heark'e, my Dear.

Takes PLUME *to one side of the Stage, and entertains him in dumb Show.*

KITE. Sir, he in the plain Coat is Captain *Plume*, I'm his Serjeant, and will take my Oath on't.

SILVIA. What! Are you Serjeant *Kite*?

KITE. At your Service.

SILVIA. Then I wou'd not take your Oath for a Farthing.

KITE. A very understanding Youth of his Age! Pray Sir, let me look you full in the Face.

SILVIA. Well, Sir, what have you to say to my Face?

KITE. The very Image and Superscription of my Brother, two Bullets of the same Caliber were never so like; sure it must be *Charles, Charles*——

SILVIA. What d'ye mean by *Charles*?

KITE. The Voice too, only a little Variation in Effa ut flat; my dear Brother, for I must call you so if you shou'd have the Fortune to enter into the most Noble Society of the Sword, I bespeak you for a Comrade.

SILVIA. No, Sir, I'll be your Captain's Comrade if any body's.

KITE. Ambition! There again, 'tis a noble Passion for a Soldier; by that I gain'd this glorious Halberd. Ambition! I see a Commission in his Face already, pray noble Captain give me leave to salute you.

Offers to kiss her.

SILVIA. What! Men kiss one another!

KITE. We Officers do, 'tis our way; we live together like Man and Wife, always either kissing or fighting——But I see a Storm a coming.

SILVIA. Now, Serjeant, I shall see who is your Captain by your knocking down the t'other.

KITE. My Captain scorns Assistance, Sir.

BRAZEN. How dare you contend for any thing, and not dare to draw your Sword? But you're a young Fellow, and have not been much abroad, I excuse that; but prithee resign the Man, prithee do, you're a very honest Fellow.

PLUME. You lye, and you're a Son of a Whore.

Draws and makes up to BRAZEN.

BRAZEN. ⟨*Retiring.*⟩ Hold, hold, did you not refuse to fight for the Lady?

PLUME. I always do, but for a Man I'll fight Knee deep, so you lye again.

PLUME *and* BRAZEN *fight a Traverse or two about the Stage;* SILVIA *draws, and is held by* KITE, *who sounds to Arms with his Mouth, takes* SILVIA *in his Arms, and carries her off the Stage.*

BRAZEN. Hold——Where's the Man?

PLUME. Gone.

BRAZEN. Then what do we fight for? ⟨*Puts up.*⟩ Now let's embrace, my Dear.

PLUME. With all my heart, my Dear. ⟨*Puts up.*⟩ I suppose *Kite* has listed him by this time. *They embrace.*

BRAZEN. You're a brave Fellow, I always fight with a Man before I make him my Friend; and if once I find he will fight, I never quarrel with him afterwards——And now I'll tell you a Secret, my dear Friend, that Lady that we frighted out o' the Walk just now I found in Bed this Morning, so beautiful, so inviting——I presently lock'd the Door——But I'm a Man of Honour——But I believe I shall marry her nevertheless; her twenty thousand Pound you know will be a pretty Convenience, I had an Assignation with her here, but your coming spoil'd my Sport, curse ye, my Dear,——But don't do so again.

PLUME. No, no, my dear, Men are my Business at present.

Exeunt.

ACT IV

SCENE I

SCENE, *of the Walk continues*

ROSE *and* BULLOCK *meeting.*

ROSE. Where have you been, you great Booby, you're always out o'th' way in the time of Preferment?

BULLOCK. Preferment! who shou'd prefer me?

ROSE. I wou'd prefer you, who shou'd prefer a Man but a Woman? Come throw away that great Club, hold up your Head, cock your Hat, and look big.

BULLOCK. Ah! *Ruose, Ruose,* I fear somebody will look big sooner than Folk think of; this genteel Breeding never comes into the Country without a Train of Followers.——Here has been *Cartwheel* your Sweet-heart, what will become o' him?

ROSE. Look'e, I'm a great Woman, and will provide for my Relations; I told the Captain how finely he could play upon the Tabor and Pipe, so he has set him down for a Drum-Major.

BULLOCK. Nay, Sister, why did not you keep that Place for me? You know I always lov'd to be a drumming, if it were but on a Table, or on a Quart Pot.

Enter SILVIA.

SILVIA. Had I but a Commission in my Pocket I fancy my Breeches wou'd become me as well as any ranting Fellow of 'um all; for I take a bold Step, a rakish Toss, a smart Cock, and an impudent Air to be the principal Ingredients in the Composition of a Captain.——What's here, *Rose,* my Nurse's Daughter? I'll go and practice——Come, Child, kiss me at once. ⟨*Kisses* ROSE.⟩ And her Brother too!——Well, honest Dungfork, do you know the Difference between a Horse Cart, and a Cart Horse, eh?

BULLOCK. I presume that your Worship is a Captain by your Cloaths and your Courage.

SILVIA. Suppose I were, wou'd you be contented to list, Friend?

ROSE. No, no, tho' your Worship be a handsome Man, there be others as fine as you; my Brother is engag'd to Captain *Plume.*

SILVIA. *Plume!* do you know Captain *Plume*?

ROSE. Yes, I do, and he knows me.——He took the very Ribbands out of his Shirt Sleeves, and put them into my Shoes.——See there——I can assure you I can do any thing with the Captain.

BULLOCK. That is, in a modest way, Sir.——Have a care what you say, *Ruose*, don't shame your Parentage.

ROSE. Nay, for that matter I am not so simple as to say that I can do any thing with the Captain, but what I may do with any body else.

SILVIA. Soh!——and pray what do you expect from this Captain, Child?

ROSE. I expect, Sir! I expect,——but he order'd me to tell no body——but suppose that he shou'd promise to marry me.

SILVIA. You shou'd have a care, my Dear, Men will promise any thing before-hand.

ROSE. I know that, but he promis'd to marry me afterwards.

BULLOCK. Wauns, *Ruose*, what have you said?

SILVIA. Afterwards! after what?

ROSE. After I had sold him my Chickens,——I hope there's no Harm in that, tho' there be an ugly Song of Chickens and Sparragus.

Enter PLUME.

PLUME. What! Mr. *Wilfull*, so close with my Market Woman!

SILVIA. I'll try if he loves her. ⟨*Aside.*⟩ Close, Sir! ay, and closer yet, Sir——Come, my pretty Maid, you and I will withdraw a little——

PLUME. No, no, Friend, I han't done with her yet.

SILVIA. Nor have I begun with her, so I have as good a Right as you have.

PLUME. Thou art a bloody impudent Fellow——let her go, I say.

SILVIA. Do you let her go.

PLUME. *Entendez vous Francois, mon petit Garson.*

SILVIA. *Ouy.*

PLUME. *Si voulez vous donc vous enroller dans ma Companie, la damoiselle sera a vous.*

SILVIA. *Avez vous couche avec elle.*

PLUME. *Non.*

SILVIA. *Assurement?*

PLUME. *Ma foi.*

SILVIA. *C'est assez——Je serai votre soldat.*

PLUME. *La prenez donc*——I'll change a Woman for a Man at any time.

ROSE. But I hope, Captain, you won't part with me. ⟨*Crys.*⟩ I have heard before indeed that you Captains use to sell your Men.

BULLOCK. ⟨*Crying.*⟩ Pray, Captain, don't send *Ruose* to the *West-Indies.*

PLUME. Ha, ha, ha, *West-Indies*! no, no, my honest Lad, give me thy Hand, nor you, nor she shall move a step farther than I do. ——This Gentleman is one of us, and will be kind to you, Mrs. *Rose.*

ROSE. But will you be so kind to me, Sir, as the Captain wou'd?

SILVIA. I can't be altogether so kind to you, my Circumstances are not so good as the Captain's——but I'll take care of you, upon my Word.

PLUME. Ay, ay, we'll all take care of her,——She shall live like a Princess, and her Brother here shall be——what wou'd you be?

BULLOCK. Ah! Sir, if you had not promis'd the Place of Drum-Major.

PLUME. Ay, that is promis'd——but what think ye of Barrack-Master? You're a Person of Understanding, and Barrack-Master you shall be.——But what's become of this same *Cartwheel* you told me of, my dear?

ROSE. We'll go fetch him——Come, Brother Barrack-Master ——We shall find you at home, noble Captain?

Exit ROSE *and* BULLOCK.

PLUME. Yes, yes——and now, Sir, here are your forty Shillings.

SILVIA. Captain *Plume*, I despise your Listing-money, if I do serve, 'tis purely for Love——of that Wench I mean; for you must know, that among my other Sallies, I have spent the best part of my Fortune in search of a Maid, and cou'd never find one hitherto; so you may be assur'd that I won't sell my Freedom under a less Purchase than I did my Estate,——so before I list I must be certify'd that this Girl is a Virgin.

PLUME. Mr. *Wilfull*, I can't tell how you can be certify'd in that point, till you try, but upon my Honour she may be a Vestal for ought that I know to the contrary.——I gain'd her Heart indeed by some trifling Presents and Promises, and knowing that the best Security for a Woman's Soul is her Body, I wou'd have made my self Master of that too, had not the Jealousie of my impertinent Landlady interpos'd.

SILVIA. So you only want an Opportunity for accomplishing your Designs upon her.

PLUME. Not at all, I have already gain'd my Ends, which were only the drawing in one or two of her Followers; the Women, you know, are the Loadstones every where——gain the Wives, and you're caress'd by the Husbands; please the Mistresses, and you are valu'd by their Gallants; secure an Interest with the finest Women at Court, and you procure the Favour of the Greatest Men: So kiss the prettiest Country Wenches, and you are sure of listing the lustiest Fellows. Some People may call this Artifice, but I term it Stratagem, since it is so main a part of the Service——Besides, the Fatigues of Recruiting is so intollerable, that unless we cou'd make our selves some Pleasure amidst the Pain, no mortal Man wou'd be able to bear it.

SILVIA. Well, Sir, I'm satisfy'd as to the Point in Debate——But now let me beg you to lay aside your Recruiting Airs, put on the Man of Honour, and tell me plainly what Usage I must expect when I'm under your Command.

PLUME. You must know in the first place then, that I hate to have Gentlemen in my Company, for they are always troublesome and expensive, sometimes dangerous; and 'tis a constant Maxim among us, That those who know the least, obey the best.——Notwithstanding all this, I find something so agreeable about you, that engages me to court your Company; and I can't tell how it is, but I shou'd be uneasy to see you under the Command of any body else.——Your Usage will chiefly depend upon your Behaviour, only this you must expect, that if you commit a small Fault I will excuse it, if a great one, I'll discharge you, for something tells me I shall not be able to punish you.

SILVIA. And something tells me, that if you do discharge me, 'twill be the greatest Punishment you will inflict; for were we this moment to go upon the greatest Dangers in your Profession, they wou'd be less terrible to me, than to stay behind you.——And now your Hand,——this lists me——and now you are my Captain.

PLUME. Your Friend—— ⟨*Kisses her.*⟩ 'Sdeath! there's something in this Fellow that charms me.

SILVIA. One Favour I must beg——This Affair will make some Noise, and I have some Friends that wou'd censure my Conduct if I threw my self into the Circumstances of a private Centinel of my own Head, I must therefore take care to be impress'd by the Act of Parliament, you shall leave that to me——

PLUME. What you please as to that——Will you lodge at my Quarters in the mean time? You shall have part of my Bed.

SILVIA. O fie, lye with a Common Soldier!——wou'd not you rather lye with a common Woman?

PLUME. No, Faith, I am not that Rake that the World imagines, I have got an Air of Freedom, which People mistake for Lewdness in me, as they mistake Formality in others for Religion; the World is all a Cheat, only I take mine which is undesign'd to be more excusable than theirs, which is hypocritical; I hurt no body but my self, and they abuse all Mankind——Will you lye with me?

SILVIA. No, no, Captain, you forget *Rose*, she's to be my Bed-Fellow you know.

PLUME. I had forgot, pray be kind to her.

Exeunt severally.

Enter MELINDA *and* LUCY.

MELINDA. 'Tis the greatest Misfortune in Nature for a Woman to want a Confident, we are so weak that we can do nothing without Assistance, and then a Secret racks us worse than the Cholick; I'm at this Minute so sick of a Secret, that I'm ready to faint away——help me, *Lucy*.

LUCY. Bless me, Madam, what's the matter?

MELINDA. Vapours only——I begin to recover——if *Silvia* were in Town, I cou'd heartily forgive her Faults for the Ease of discovering my own.

LUCY. You're thoughtful, Madam, am not I worthy to know the Cause?

MELINDA. You're a Servant, and a Secret wou'd make you saucy.

LUCY. Not unless you shou'd find fault without a Cause, Madam.

MELINDA. Cause or not Cause, I must not lose the Pleasure of chiding when I please; Women must discharge their Vapours some where, and before we get Husbands, our Servants must expect to bear with 'um.

LUCY. Then, Madam, you had better raise me to a degree above a Servant, you know my Family, and that five hundred Pound wou'd set me upon the Foot of a Gentlewoman, and make me worthy the Confidence of any Lady in the Land; besides, Madam, 'twill extremely encourage me in the great Design that I now have in hand.

MELINDA. I don't find that your Design can be of any great Advantage to you, 'twill please me indeed in the Humour I have of being reveng'd on the Fool for his Vanity of making Love to me, so I don't much care if I do promise you five hundred Pound the Day of my Marriage.

LUCY. That is the way, Madam, to make me diligent in the Vocation of a Confident, which I think is generally to bring People together.

MELINDA. O, *Lucy*, I can hold my Secret no longer——You must know that hearing of the famous Fortune-teller in Town, I went disguis'd to satisfie a Curiosity which has cost me dear; that Fellow is certainly the Devil, or one of his Bosom-Favourites, he has told me the most surprising things of my past Life——

LUCY. Things past, Madam, can hardly be reckon'd surprising, because we know them already; did he tell you any thing surprising that was to come.

MELINDA. One thing very surprising, he said I shou'd die a Maid.

LUCY. Die a Maid——Come into the World for nothing! Dear Madam, if you shou'd believe him, it might come to pass; for the bare Thought on't might kill one in four and twenty Hours——And did you ask him any Questions about me?

MELINDA. You! Why, I pass'd for you.

LUCY. So 'tis I that am to die a Maid——But the Devil was a

Lyar from the beginning, he can't make me die a Maid——I have put it out of his Power already.

MELINDA. I do but jest, I wou'd have pass'd for you, and call'd my self *Lucy*, but he presently told me my Name, my Quality, my Fortune, and gave me the whole History of my Life; he told me of a Lover I had in this Country, and describ'd *Worthy* exactly, but in nothing so well as in his present Indifference——I fled to him for Refuge here to day——He never so much as incourag'd me in my Fright, but coldly told me that he was sorry for the Accident, because it might give the Town cause to censure my Conduct; excus'd his not waiting on me home, made me a careless Bow, and walk'd off. 'Sdeath, I cou'd have stabb'd him, or my self, 'twas the same thing——Yonder he comes——I will so slave him.

LUCY. Don't exasperate him, consider what the Fortune-teller told you, Men are scarce; and as Times go, it is not impossible for a Woman to die a Maid.

Enter WORTHY.

MELINDA. No matter.

WORTHY. I find she's warm'd, I must strike while the Iron is hot,——You have a great deal of Courage, Madam, to venture into the Walks where you were so late frightened.

MELINDA. And you have a Quantity of Impudence to appear before me, that you have so lately affronted.

WORTHY. I had no design to affront you, nor appear before you either, Madam; I left you here, because I had Business in another Place, and came hither thinking to meet another Person.

MELINDA. Since you find your self disappointed, I hope you'll withdraw to another part of the Walk.

WORTHY. The Walk is as free for me as you, Madam, and broad enough for us both. ⟨*They walk one by another, he with his Hat cockt, she fretting and tearing her Fan.*⟩ Will you please to take Snuff, Madam. ⟨*He offers her his Box, she strikes it out of his hand, while he is gathering it up, enter* BRAZEN *who takes* MELINDA *about the Middle, she cuffs him.*⟩

BRAZEN. What! Here before me! My Dear.

MELINDA. What means this Insolence?

LUCY. ⟨*Runs to* BRAZEN.⟩ Are you mad? Don't you see Mr. *Worthy*?

BRAZEN. No, no, I'm struck blind——*Worthy*! Adso, well turn'd, my Mistress has Wit at her Fingers ends——Madam, I ask your pardon, 'tis our way abroad——Mr. *Worthy*, you're the happy Man.

WORTHY. I don't envy your Happiness very much, if the Lady can afford no other sort of Favours but what she has bestow'd upon you.

MELINDA. I'm sorry the Favour miscarry'd, for it was design'd for you, Mr. *Worthy*; and be assur'd, 'tis the last and only Favour you must expect at my hands——Captain, I ask your Pardon——

Exit with LUCY.

BRAZEN. I grant it——You see, Mr. *Worthy*, 'twas only a random shot, it might ha' taken off your Head as well as mine——Courage, my Dear, 'tis the Fortune of War——But the Enemy has thought fit to withdraw, I think.

WORTHY. Withdraw! Oons, Sir, what d'ye mean by withdraw?

BRAZEN. I'll show you.

Exit.

WORTHY. She's lost, irrecoverably lost, and *Plume*'s Advice has ruin'd me; 'sdeath, why shou'd I that knew her haughty Spirit be rul'd by a Man that is a Stranger to her Pride.

Enter PLUME.

PLUME. Ha, ha, ha, a Battel Royal; don't frown so, Man, she's your own, I tell'e; I saw the Fury of her Love in the Extremity of her Passion, the Wildness of her Anger is a certain sign that she loves you to Madness; that Rogue, *Kite*, began the Battel with abundance of Conduct, and will bring you off victorious, my Life on't; he plays his Part admirably, she's to be with him again presently.

WORTHY. But what cou'd be the meaning of *Brazen*'s Familiarity with her.

PLUME. You are no Logician if you pretend to draw Consequences from the Actions of Fools, there's no arguing by the Rule of Reason upon a Silence without Principles, and such is their Conduct; Whim, unaccountable Whim, hurries them on, like a Man drunk with Brandy before ten a Clock in the Morning ——But we lose our sport, *Kite* has open'd above an Hour ago, let's away.

Exeunt.

SCENE II

SCENE, *A Chamber, a Table with Books and Globes.*

KITE *disguis'd in a strange Habit, and sitting at the Table.*

KITE. ⟨*Rising.*⟩ By the Position of the Heavens, gain'd from my Observation upon these Celestial Globes, I find that *Luna* was a Tide-waiter, *Sol* a Surveyor, *Mercury* a Thief, *Venus* a Whore, *Saturn* an Alderman, *Jupiter* a Rake, and *Mars* a Serjeant of Granadeers——And this is the Sistem of *Kite* the Conjurer.

Enter PLUME *and* WORTHY.

PLUME. Well, what Success?

KITE. I have sent away a Shoemaker and a Taylor already, one's to be a Captain of Marines, and the other a Major of Dragoons, I am to manage them at Night——Have you seen the Lady Mr. *Worthy*?

WORTHY. Ay, but it won't do——Have you show'd her her Name that I tore off from the bottom of the Letter?

KITE. No, Sir, I reserve that for the last stroak.

PLUME. What Letter?

WORTHY. One that I wou'd not let you see, for fear you shou'd break *Melinda*'s Windows in good earnest.

Knocking at the Door.

KITE. Officers to your Post——

Exeunt WORTHY *and* PLUME.

Ticho, mind the Door. ⟨*Servant opens the Door, and enter a Smith.*⟩

SMITH. Well, Master, are you the cunning Man?

KITE. I am the learn'd *Copernicus.*

SMITH. Well, Master *Coppernose*, I'm but a poor Man, and I can't afford above a Shilling for my Fortune.

KITE. Perhaps, that is more than 'tis worth.

SMITH. Look'e, Doctor, Let me have something that's good for my Shilling, or I'll have my Money again.

KITE. If there be Faith in the Stars, you shall have your Shilling forty fold. You're hand, Countryman——You are by Trade a Smith.

SMITH. How the Devil shou'd you know that?

KITE. Because the Devil and you are Brother Tradesmen—— You were born under *Forceps*.

SMITH. *Forceps!* What's that?

KITE. One of the Signs; there's *Leo, Sagitarius, Forceps, Furns, Dixmude, Namur, Brussels, Charleroy*, and so forth——Twelve of 'em——Let me see——Did you ever make any Bombs or Cannons Bullets.

SMITH. Not I.

KITE. You either have, or will——The Stars have decreed, that you shall be——I must have more Money, Sir, your Fortune's great——

SMITH. Faith, Doctor, I have no more.

KITE. O, Sir, I'll trust you, and take it out of your Arrears.

SMITH. Arrears! What Arrears?

KITE. The five hundred Pound that's owing to you from the Government.

SMITH. Owing me!

KITE. Owing you, Sir——Let me see your t'other hand——I beg your pardon, it will be owing to you; and the Rogue of an Agent will demand fifty *per Cent.* for a Fortnight's Advance.

SMITH. I'm in the Clouds, Doctor, all this while.

KITE. So am I, Sir, among the Stars——In two Years, three Months, and two Hours, you will be made Captain of the Forges to the grand Train of Artillery, and will have ten Shillings a Day, and two Servants; 'tis the Decree of the Stars, and of the fix'd Stars, that are as immoveable as your Anvil——Strike, Sir, while the Iron is hot——Fly, Sir, be gone——

SMITH. What, what wou'd you have me do, Doctor? I wish the Stars wou'd put me in a way for this fine Place.

KITE. The Stars do——Let me see——Ay, about an Hour hence walk carelessly into the Market-place, and you'll see a tall slender Gentleman cheapning a Pen'worth of Apples, with a Cane hanging upon his Button——This Gentleman will ask you——What's a Clock——He's your Man, and the Maker of your Fortune; follow him, follow him: And now go home, and take leave of your Wife and Children——An Hour hence exactly is your time——

SMITH. A tall slender Gentleman you say! With a Cane, pray what sort of a Head has the Cane?

KITE. An Amber Head, with a black Ribband.

SMITH. But pray, of what Employment is the Gentleman?

KITE. Let me see——He's either a Collector of the Excise, a Plenipotentiary, or a Captain of Granadeers——I can't tell exactly which——But he'll call you honest——Your Name is——

SMITH. *Thomas.*

KITE. Right, he'll call you honest *Tom*——

SMITH. But how the Devil shou'd he know my Name?

KITE. O, there are several sorts of *Toms*——*Tom a Lincoln, Tom-tit, Tom Telltroth, Tom o' Bedlam, Tom Fool*——⟨*Knocking at the Door.*⟩ Be gone——An Hour hence precisely——

SMITH. You say he'll ask me what's a Clock?

KITE. Most certainly, and you'll answer——You don't know, and be sure you look at St. *Mary's* Dial, for the Sun won't shine, and if it shou'd, you won't be able to tell the Figures.

SMITH. I will, I will.

Exit.

PLUME. ⟨*Behind.*⟩ Well done, Conjurer, go on and prosper.

KITE. As you were.

Enter a Butcher.

KITE. What! My old Friend *Pluck*, the Butcher—— ⟨*Aside.*⟩ I offer'd the surly Bull-dog five Guineas this Morning, and he refus'd it.

BUTCHER. So, Master Conjurer——Here's half a Crown——And now you must understand——

KITE. Hold, Friend, I know your Business beforehand.

BUTCHER. You're devilish cunning then; for I don't well know it my self.

KITE. I know more than you, Friend——You have a foolish Saying, that such a one knows no more than the Man-in-the-Moon; I tell you the Man in the Moon knows more than all the Men under the Sun, don't the Moon see all the World?

BUTCHER. All the World see the Moon, I must confess.

KITE. Then she must see all the World, that's certain——Give me your hand——You are by Trade either a Butcher or a Surgeon.

BUTCHER. True——I am a Butcher.

KITE. And a Surgeon you will be, the Employments differ only in the Name——He that can cut up an Ox, may dissect a Man; and the same Dexterity that cracks a Marrow-bone, will cut off a Leg or an Arm.

BUTCHER. What d'ye mean, Doctor, what d'ye mean?

KITE. Patience, Patience, Mr. Surgeon General, the Stars are great Bodies, and move slowly.

BUTCHER. But what d'ye mean by Surgeon General, Doctor?

KITE. Nay, Sir, if your Worship won't have Patience, I must beg the Favour of your Worship's absence.

BUTCHER. My Worship, my Worship! But why my Worship?

KITE. Nay, then I have done.

Sits.

BUTCHER. Pray, Doctor.

KITE. Fire and Fury, Sir, ⟨*Rises in a Passion*⟩ do you think the Stars will be hurry'd——Do the Stars owe you any Money, Sir, that you dare to dun their Lordships at this rate——Sir, I am Porter to the Stars, and I am order'd to let no Dun come near their Doors.

BUTCHER. Dear Doctor, I never had any Dealings with the Stars, they don't owe me a Penny——But since you are the Porter, please to accept of this Half Crown to drink their Healths, and don't be angry.

KITE. Let me see your hand, then, once more——Here has been Gold——Five Guineas, my Friend, in this very hand this Morning.

BUTCHER. Nay, then he is the Devil——Pray, Doctor, were you born of a Woman, or did you come into the World of your own Head?

KITE. That's a Secret——This Gold was offer'd you by a proper handsome Man call'd *Hawk*, or *Buzzard*, or——

BUTCHER. *Kite* you mean.

KITE. Ay, ay, *Kite*.

BUTCHER. As errant a Rogue as ever carry'd a Halbard——the impudent Rascal wou'd have decoy'd me for a Soldier.

KITE. A Soldier! A Man of your Substance for a Soldier! Your Mother has a hundred Pound in hard Money lying at this Minute in the hands of a Mercer, not forty Yards from this Place.

BUTCHER. Oons, and so she has; but very few know so much.

KITE. I know it, and that Rogue, what's his Name, *Kite*, knew it? And offer'd you five Guineas to list, because he knew your poor Mother wou'd give the hundred for your Discharge——

BUTCHER. There's a Dog now——'Flesh, Doctor, I'll give you t'other half Crown, and tell me that this same *Kite* will be hang'd.

KITE. He's in as much Danger as any Man in the County of *Salop*.

BUTCHER. There's you're Fee——But you have forgot the Surgeon General all this while.

KITE. You put the Stars in a Passion. ⟨*Looks on his Books.*⟩ But now they're pacify'd again——Let me see——Did you never cut off a Man's Leg?

BUTCHER. No.

KITE. Recollect, pray.

BUTCHER. I say no.

KITE. That's strange, wonderful strange; but nothing is strange to me, such wonderful Changes have I seen——The second, or third, ay, the third Campaign that you make in *Flanders*, the Leg of a great Officer will be shatter'd by a great Shot; you will be there accidentally, and with your Cleaver chop off the Limb at a Blow: In short, the Operation will be perform'd with so much Dexterity, that with the general Applause you will be made Surgeon General of the whole Army.

BUTCHER. Nay, for the matter of cutting off a Limb——I'll do't——I'll do't with any Surgeon in *Europe*, but I have no Thoughts of making a Campaign.

KITE. You have no Thoughts! What matter for your Thoughts? The Stars have decreed it, and you must go.

BUTCHER. The Stars decree it! Oons, Sir, the Justices can't press me.

KITE. Nay, Friend, 'tis none of my Business, I ha' done——Only mind this——You'll know more an Hour and a half hence ——That's all——Farewel.

Going.

BUTCHER. Hold, hold, Doctor, Surgeon General! Pray what is the Place worth, pray.

KITE. Five hundred Pound a Year, beside Guineas for Claps.

BUTCHER. Five hundred Pound a Year!——An Hour and half hence you say?

KITE. Prithee Friend be quiet, don't be so troublesome——Here's such a Work to make a Booby Butcher accept of five hundred Pound a Year——But if you must hear it——I tell you in short, you'll be standing in your Stall an Hour and half hence, and a Gentleman will come by with a Snuff-box in his hand, and the tip of his Handkerchief hanging out of his right Pocket——He'll ask you the Price of a Loyn of Veal, and at the same time stroak your great Dog upon the Head, and call him *Chopper*.

BUTCHER. Mercy upon us——*Chopper* is the Dog's Name.

KITE. Look'e there——What I say is true, things that are to come must come to pass——Get you home, sell off your Stock, don't mind the whining and the snivelling of your Mother and your Sister, Women always hinder Preferment; make what Money you can, and follow that Gentleman——His Name begins with a P—— Mind that——There will be the Barber's Daughter too, that you promis'd Marriage to, she will be pulling and haleing you to pieces.

BUTCHER. What! know *Sally* too? He's the Devil, and he needs must go that the Devil drives—— 〈*Going.*〉 The tip of his Handkerchief out of his left Pocket?

KITE. No, no, his right Pocket, if it be the left, 'tis none of the Man.

BUTCHER. Well, well, I'll mind him.

Exit.

PLUME. 〈*Behind with his Pocket-book.*〉 The right Pocket, you say?

KITE. I hear the rustling of Silks. 〈*Knocking.*〉 Fly, Sir, 'tis Madam *Melinda*.

Enter MELINDA *and* LUCY.

KITE. *Tycho,* Chairs for the Ladies.

MELINDA. Don't trouble your self, we shan't stay, Doctor.

KITE. Your Ladyship is to stay much longer than you imagine.

MELINDA. For what?

KITE. For a Husband——For your part, Madam, 〈*To* LUCY〉 you won't stay for a Husband.

LUCY. Pray, Doctor, do you converse with the Stars, or with the Devil?

KITE. With both; when I have the Destinies of Men in search, I consult the Stars, when the Affairs of Women come under my hand, I advise with my t'other Friend.

MELINDA. And have you rais'd the Devil upon my account?

KITE. Yes, Madam, and he's now under the Table.

LUCY. Oh! Heavens protect us——dear Madam, let us be gone.

KITE. If you be afraid of him, why do you come to consult him?

MELINDA. Don't fear, Fool. Do you think, Sir, that because I'm a Woman I'm to be fool'd out of my Reason, or frighted out of my Senses?——Come, show me this Devil.

KITE. He's a little busie at present, but when he has done he shall wait on you.

MELINDA. What is he doing?

KITE. Writing your Name in his Pocket-book.

MELINDA. Ha, ha, ha, my Name! pray what have you or he to do with my Name?

KITE. Look'e, fair Lady,——the Devil is a very modest Person, he seeks no body unless they seek him first; he's chain'd up like a Mastiff, and cannot stir unless he be let loose.——You come to me to have your Fortune told——do you think, Madam, that I can answer you of my own Head? No, Madam, the Affairs of Women are so irregular, that nothing less than the Devil can give any account of 'em. Now to convince you of your Incredulity, I'll show you a Tryal of my Skill.——Here, you, *Cacodemon del fuego*, exert your Power,——draw me this Lady's Name, the word *Melinda* in the proper Letters and Character of her own hand writing.——Do it at three Motions,——one, two, three 'tis done——Now, Madam, will you please to send your Maid to fetch it.

LUCY. I fetch it! the Devil fetch me if I do.

MELINDA. My Name in my own Hand-writing! that wou'd be convincing indeed.

KITE. Seeing's believing. 〈*Goes to the Table, lifts up the Carpet.*〉 Here *Tre, Tre,* poor *Tre,* give me the Bone, Sirrah——Oh! oh! the Devil, the Devil in good earnest, my Hand, my Hand, the Devil, my Hand! ⟨*He puts his Hand under the Table,* PLUME *steals to the other side of the Table and catches him by the Hand.* MELINDA *and* LUCY *shriek, and run to a Corner of the Stage.*—— KITE *discovers* PLUME, *and gets away his Hand.*⟩ A plague o' your Pincers, he has fixt his Nails in my very Flesh. Oh! Madam, you put the Demon into such a Passion with your Scruples, that it has almost cost me my Hand.

MELINDA. It has cost us our Lives almost——but have you got the Name?

KITE. Got it! Ay, Madam, I have got it here——I'm sure the Blood comes——but there's your Name upon that square piece of Paper——behold——

MELINDA. 'Tis wonderful——My very Letters to a tittle.

LUCY. 'Tis like your Hand, Madam, but not so like your Hand, neither, and now I look nearer, 'tis not like your Hand at all.

KITE. Here's a Chamber-maid now that will out-lie the Devil.

LUCY. Look'e, Madam, they shan't impose upon us, People can't remember their Hands no more than they can their Faces—— Come, Madam, let us be certain, write your Name upon this Paper—— ⟨*Takes out Paper and folds it*⟩ then we'll compare the two Names.

KITE. Any thing for your Satisfaction, Madam,——Here's Pen and Ink——

MELINDA *writes, and* LUCY *holds the Paper.*

LUCY. Let me see it, Madam, 'tis the same, the very same.—— ⟨*Aside.*⟩ But I'll secure one Copy for my own Affairs.

MELINDA. This is Demonstration.

KITE. 'Tis so, Madam, the word Demonstration comes from Demon the Father of Lies.

MELINDA. Well, Doctor, I'm convinc'd; and now pray what account can you give me of my future Fortune?

KITE. Before the Sun has made one Course round this earthly Globe, your Fortune will be fixt for Happiness or Misery.

MELINDA. What! so near the Crisis of my Fate!

KITE. Let me see——about the Hour of Ten to Morrow Morning you will be saluted by a Gentleman who will come to take his Leave of you, being design'd for Travel. His Intention of going abroad is sudden, and the Occasion a Woman. Your Fortune and his are like the Bullet and the Barrel, one runs plump into the t'other——in short, if the Gentleman travels he will die abroad; and if he does you will die before he comes home.

MELINDA. What sort of Man is he?

KITE. Madam, he is a fine Gentleman, and a Lover——that is, a Man of very good Sense, and a very great Fool.

MELINDA. How is that possible, Doctor?

KITE. Because, Madam,——because it is so: A Woman's Reason is the best for a Man's being a Fool.

MELINDA. Ten a Clock you say.

KITE. Ten, about the Hour of Tea drinking throughout the Kingdom.

MELINDA. Here, Doctor. 〈*Gives him Money.*〉 *Lucy*, have you any Questions to ask?

LUCY. O! Madam, a thousand.

KITE. I must beg your Patience till another time, for I expect more Company this Minute; besides, I must discharge the Gentleman under the Table.

LUCY. Pray, Sir, discharge us first.

KITE. *Tycho*, wait on the Ladies down Stairs.

Ex. MELINDA *and* LUCY.

Enter PLUME *and* WORTHY *laughing.*

KITE. Ay, you may well laugh, Gentlemen, not all the Cannon of the *French* Army cou'd have frighted me so much as that Gripe you gave me under the Table.

PLUME. I think, Mr. Doctor, I out-conjur'd you that bout.

KITE. I was surpriz'd, for I shou'd not have taken a Captain for a Conjurer.

PLUME. No more than I shou'd a Serjeant for a Wit.

KITE. Mr. *Worthy*, you were pleas'd to wish me Joy to Day, I hope to be able to return the Complement to Morrow.

WORTHY. I'll make it the best Complement to you that you ever made in your Life, if you do; but I must be a Traveller you say?

KITE. No farther than the Chops of the Channel, I presume, Sir.

PLUME. That we have concerted already. 〈*Knocking hard.*〉 Hey day! you don't profess Midwifery, Doctor?

KITE. Away to your Ambuscade.

Exeunt PLUME *and* WORTHY.

Enter BRAZEN.

BRAZEN. Your Servant, Servant, my dear.

KITE. Stand off——I have my Familiar already.

BRAZEN. Are you bewitch'd, my dear?

KITE. Yes, my dear, but mine is a peaceful Spirit, and hates Gunpowder——thus I fortify my self, ⟨*Draws a Circle round him*⟩ and now, Captain, have a care how you force my Lines.

BRAZEN. Lines! what dost talk of Lines? You have something like a Fishing Rod there, indeed; but I come to be acquainted with you, Man——what's your Name, my dear?

KITE. *Conundrum.*

BRAZEN. *Conundrum!* rat me, I know a famous Doctor in *London* of your Name, where were you born?

KITE. I was born in *Algebra.*

BRAZEN. *Algebra!*——'Tis no Country in *Christendom* I'm sure, unless it be some pitiful Place in the Highlands of *Scotland.*

KITE. Right! I told you I was bewitch'd.

BRAZEN. So am I, my dear, I'm going to be marry'd.——I've had two Letters from a Lady of Fortune that Loves me to Madness, Fits, Chollick, Spleen, and Vapours——Shall I marry her in four and twenty Hours, ay or no?

KITE. I must have the Year and Day o'th' Month when these Letters were dated.

BRAZEN. Why, you old Bitch, did you ever hear of Love Letters dated with the Year and Day o'th' Month, do you think Billets Deux are like Bank Bills?

KITE. They are not so good——but if they bear no Date, I must examine the Contents.

BRAZEN. Contents, that you shall, old Boy, here they be both.

KITE. Only the last you receiv'd, if you please. ⟨*Takes the letter.*⟩ Now Sir, if you please to let me consult my Books for a Minute, I'll send this Letter inclos'd to you with the Determination of the Stars upon it to your Lodgings.

BRAZEN. With all my Heart——I must give him—— ⟨*Puts his Hand in's Pocket.*⟩ *Algebra!* I fancy, Doctor, 'tis hard to calculate the Place of your Nativity——Here—— ⟨*Gives him Money*⟩ and if I succeed, I'll build a Watch-Tower upon the top of the highest Mountain in *Wales* for the Study of Astrology, and the Benefit of *Conundrums*.

Exit.

Enter PLUME *and* WORTHY.

WORTHY. O! Doctor, that Letter's worth a Million, let me see it——and now I have it, I'm afraid to open it.

PLUME. Pho, let me see it, ⟨*Opening the Letter.*⟩ if she be a Jilt——Damn her, she is one——there's her Name at the bottom on't.

WORTHY. How!——then I will travel in good earnest——by all my hopes, 'tis *Lucy*'s Hand.

PLUME. *Lucy*'s!

WORTHY. Certainly, 'tis no more like *Melinda*'s Character than black is to white.

PLUME. Then 'tis certainly *Lucy*'s Contrivance to draw in *Brazen* for a Husband——but are you sure 'tis not *Melinda*'s Hand?

WORTHY. You shall see, where's the bit of Paper I gave you just now that the Devil writ *Melinda* upon.

KITE. Here, Sir.

PLUME. 'Tis plain, they're not the same; and is this the malicious Name that was subscrib'd to the Letter which made Mr. *Ballance* send his Daughter into the Country?

WORTHY. The very same, the other Fragments I show'd you just now I once intended it for another use, but I think I have turn'd it now to better Advantage.

PLUME. But 'twas barbarous to conceal this so long, and to continue me so many Hours in the pernicious Heresie of believing that angelick Creature cou'd change——poor *Silvia*.

WORTHY. Rich *Silvia*, you mean, and poor Captain——ha, ha, ha; come, come, Friend, *Melinda* is true, and shall be mine; *Silvia* is constant, and may be yours.

PLUME. No, she's above my Hopes——but for her sake I'll recant my Opinion of her Sex.

By some the Sex is blam'd without Design,
Light harmless Censure, such as yours and mine,
Sallies of Wit, and Vapours of our Wine.
Others the Justice of the Sex condemn,

And wanting Merit to create Esteem,
Wou'd hide their own Defects by cens'ring them.
But they secure in their all-conqu'ring Charms
Laugh at the vain Efforts of false Alarms,
He magnifies their Conquests who complains,
For none wou'd struggle were they not in Chains.

ACT V

SCENE I

SCENE, *an Antichamber, with a Perrywig, Hat and Sword upon the Table.*

Enter SILVIA *in her Night Cap.*

SILVIA. I have rested but indifferently, and I believe my Bedfellow was as little pleas'd; poor *Rose*! here she comes——

Enter ROSE.

Good morrow, my dear, how d'ye this Morning?

ROSE. Just as I was last Night, neither better nor worse for you.

SILVIA. What's the matter? did you not like your Bedfellow?

ROSE. I don't know whether I had a Bedfellow or not.

SILVIA. Did not I lye with you?

ROSE. No——I wonder you cou'd have the Conscience to ruine a poor Girl for nothing.

SILVIA. I have sav'd thee from Ruin, Child; don't be melancholy, I can give you as many fine things as the Captain can.

ROSE. But you can't I'm sure.

Knocking at the Door.

SILVIA. Odso! my Accoutrements. ⟨*Puts on her Perriwig, Hat and Sword.*⟩ Who's at the Door?

WITHOUT. Open the Door, or we'll break it down.

SILVIA. Patience a little——

Opens the Door.

Enter Constable and Mob.

CONSTABLE. We have 'um, we have 'um, the Duck and the Mallard both in the Decoy.

SILVIA. What means this Riot? Stand off ⟨*Draws*⟩ the Man dies that comes within reach of my Point.

CONSTABLE. That is not the Point, Master, put up your Sword or I shall knock you down; and so I command the Queen's Peace.

SILVIA. You are some Blockhead of a Constable.

CONSTABLE. I am so, and have a Warrant to apprehend the Bodies of you and your Whore there.

ROSE. Whore! never was poor Woman so abus'd.

Enter BULLOCK *unbutton'd.*

BULLOCK. What's matter now?——O! Mr. *Bridewell*, what brings you abroad so early?

CONSTABLE. This, Sir—— ⟨*Lays hold of* BULLOCK.⟩ You're the Queen's Prisoner.

BULLOCK. Wauns, you lye, Sir, I'm the Queen's Soldier.

CONSTABLE. No matter for that, you shall go before Justice *Ballance*.

SILVIA. *Ballance!* 'tis what I wanted——Here, Mr. Constable, I resign my Sword.

ROSE. Can't you carry us before the Captain, Mr. *Bridewell*.

CONSTABLE. Captain! ha'n't you got your Belly full of Captains yet? Come, come, make way there.

Exeunt.

SCENE II

SCENE, *Justice* BALLANCE'S *House*

BALLANCE *and* SCALE.

SCALE. I say 'tis not to be born Mr. *Ballance*.

BALLANCE. Look'e, Mr. *Scale*, for my own part I shall be very tender in what regards the Officers of the Army; they expose their Lives to so many Dangers for us Abroad, that we may give them some Grains of Allowance at Home.

SCALE. Allowance! This poor Girl's Father is my Tenant, and if I mistake not, her Mother nurst a Child for you; shall they debauch our Daughters to our Faces?

BALLANCE. Consider, Mr. *Scale*, that were it not for the Bravery of these Officers we shou'd have *French* Dragoons among us, that wou'd leave us neither Liberty, Property, Wife, nor Daughter.——Come, Mr. *Scale*, the Gentlemen are vigorous and warm, and may they continue so; the same Heat that stirs them up to Love, spurs them on to Battel: You never knew a great General in your Life that did not love a Whore——this I only speak in reference to Captain *Plume*——for the other Spark I know nothing of.

SCALE. Nor can I hear of any body that do's——O! here they come.

Enter SILVIA, BULLOCK, ROSE, *Prisoners, Constable and Mob.*

CONSTABLE. May it please your Worships, we took them in the very Act, *re infecta*, Sir; the Gentleman indeed behav'd himself like a Gentleman, for he drew his Sword and swore, and afterwards laid it down and said nothing.

BALLANCE. Give the Gentleman his Sword again——wait you without. ⟨*Exeunt Constable &c.*⟩ I'm sorry, Sir ⟨*To* SILVIA⟩ to know a Gentleman upon such Terms, that the occasion of our meeting shou'd prevent the Satisfaction of an Acquaintance.

SILVIA. Sir, you need make no Apology for your Warrant, no more than I shall do for my Behaviour.——My Innocence is upon an equal Foot with your Authority.

SCALE. Innocence! have you not seduc'd that young Maid?

SILVIA. No, Mr. Goose-Cap, she seduc'd me.

BULLOCK. So she did I'll swear,——for she propos'd Marriage first.

BALLANCE. ⟨*To* ROSE.⟩ What! then you're marry'd, Child?

ROSE. Yes, Sir, to my Sorrow.

BALLANCE. Who was Witness?

BULLOCK. That was I——I danc'd, threw the Stocking, and spoke Jokes by their Bed side I'm sure.

BALLANCE. Who was the Minister?

BULLOCK. Minister! we are Soldiers, and want no Ministers——they were marry'd by the Articles of War.

BALLANCE. Hold thy prating, Fool; your Appearance, Sir, promises some Understanding, prey, what does this Fellow mean?

SILVIA. He means Marriage, I think,——but that, you know, is so odd a thing, that hardly any two People under the Sun agree in the Ceremony; some make it a Sacrament, others a Convenience, and others make it a Jest; but among Soldiers 'tis most Sacred, our Sword, you know, is our Honour, that we lay down, the Hero jumps over it first, and the Amazon after——leap Rogue, follow Whore, the Drum beats a Ruff, and so to Bed; that's all, the Ceremony is concise.

BULLOCK. And the prettiest Ceremony, so full of Pastime and Prodigality——

BALLANCE. What! are you a Soldier?

BULLOCK. Ay, that I am——Will your Worship lend me your Cane, and I'll show you how I can exercise.

BALLANCE. 〈*Strikes him over the Head.*〉 Take it 〈*To* SILVIA.〉 Pray, Sir, what Commission may you bear?

SILVIA. I'm call'd Captain, Sir, by all the Coffee-men, Drawers, Whores and Groom Porters in *London*, for I wear a red Coat, a Sword *bien troussee*, a Martial Twist in my Cravat, a fierce Knot in my Perriwig, a Cane upon my Button; Picket in my Head, and Dice in my Pocket.

SCALE. Your Name, pray Sir.

SILVIA. Captain *Pinch*; I cock my Hat with a Pinch, I take Snuff with a Pinch, pay my Whores with a Pinch; in short, I can do any thing at a Pinch, but fight and fill my Belly.

BALLANCE. And pray, Sir, what brought you into *Shropshire*?

SILVIA. A Pinch, Sir, I knew that you Country Gentlemen want Wit, and you know that we Town Gentlemen want Money, and so——

BALLANCE. I understand you, Sir; here, Constable——

Enter Constable.

Take this Gentleman into Custody till farther Orders.

ROSE. Pray your Worship, don't be uncivil to him, for he did me no Hurt, he's the most harmless Man in the World, for all he talks so.

SCALE. Come, come, Child, I'll take care of you.

SILVIA. What, Gentlemen, rob me of my Freedom and my Wife at once! 'tis the first time they ever went together.

BALLANCE. Heark'e, Constable—— 〈*Whispers the Constable.*〉

CONSTABLE. It shall be done, Sir——Come along, Sir.

Exeunt Constable BULLOCK *and* SILVIA.

BALLANCE. Come, Mr. *Scale*, we'll manage the Spark presently.

Exeunt BALLANCE *and* SCALE.

SCENE III

SCENE, *changes to* MELINDA'S *Apartment.*

MELINDA *and* WORTHY.

MELINDA. ⟨*Aside.*⟩ So far the Prediction is right, 'tis ten exactly; and pray, Sir, how long have you been in this travelling Humour?

WORTHY. 'Tis natural, Madam, for us to avoid what disturbs our Quiet.

MELINDA. Rather the Love of Change, which is more natural, may be the Occasion of it.

WORTHY. To be sure, Madam, there must be Charms in Variety, else neither you nor I shou'd be so fond of it.

MELINDA. You mistake, Mr. *Worthy*, I am not so fond of Variety, as to travel for it; nor do I think it Prudence in you to run your self into a certain Expence and Danger, in hopes of precarious Pleasures, which at best never answer Expectation, as 'tis evident from the Example of most Travellers, that long more to return to their own Country than they did to go abroad.

WORTHY. What Pleasures I may receive abroad are indeed uncertain, but this I am sure of, I shall meet with less Cruelty among the most barbarous Nations, than I have found at home.

MELINDA. Come, Sir, you and I have been jangling a great while——I fancy if we made up our Accounts, we shou'd the sooner come to an Agreement.

WORTHY. Sure, Madam, you won't dispute your being in my Debt——My fears, Sighs, Vows, Promises, Assiduities, Anxieties, Jealousies, have run on for a whole Year, without any Payment.

MELINDA. A Year! O Mr. *Worthy*, what you owe to me is not to be paid under a seven Years Servitude; how did you use me the Year before, when taking the Advantage of my Innocence, and Necessity, you wou'd have made me your Mistress, that is, your Slave——Remember the wicked Insinuations, artful Baits, deceitful Arguments, cunning Pretences; then your impudent Behaviour, loose Expressions, familiar Letters, rude Visits, remember those, those, Mr. *Worthy*.

WORTHY. 〈*Aside.*〉 I do remember, and am sorry I made no better use of 'em. But you may remember, Madam——that——

MELINDA Sir, I'll remember nothing, 'tis your Interest that I shou'd forget; you have been barbarous to me, I have been cruel to you——Put that and that together, and let one balance the other——Now if you will begin upon a New Score, lay aside your adventering Airs, and behave your self handsomly till *Lent* be over——Here's my hand, I'll use you as a Gentlemen shou'd be.

WORTHY. And if I don't use you as a Gentlewoman shou'd be, may this be my Poyson.

Kissing her Hand.

Enter Servant.

SERVANT. Madam, the Coach is at the Door.

MELINDA. I'm going to Mr. *Ballance's* Country-house to see my Cosin *Silvia*, I have done her an Injury, and can't be easie till I have ask'd her Pardon.

WORTHY. I dare not hope for the Honour of waiting on you.

MELINDA. My Coach is full, but if you will be so Gallant as to mount your own Horses and follow us, we shall be glad to be overtaken; and if you bring Captain *Plume* with you, we shan't have the worse Reception.

WORTHY. I'll endeavour it.

Exit WORTHY *leading* MELINDA.

SCENE IV

SCENE, *The Market-Place*

PLUME *and* KITE.

PLUME. A Baker, a Taylor, a Smith, and a Butcher——I believe the first Colony planted at *Virginia* had not more Trades in their Company than I have in mine.

KITE. The Butcher, Sir, will have his hands full; for we have two Sheep-stealers among us——I hear of a Fellow too committed just now for stealing of Horses.

PLUME. We'll dispose of him among the Dragoons——Have we never a Poulterer among us?

KITE. Yes, Sir, the King of the Gypsies is a very good one, he has an excellent hand at a Goose, or a Turkey: here's Captain *Brazen*——Sir, I must go look after the Men.

Exit.

Enter BRAZEN, *reading a Letter.*

BRAZEN. Um, um, um, the Canonical Hour——Um, um, very well——My dear *Plume*! Give me a Buss.

PLUME. Half a score, if you will, my Dear; what hast got in thy hand, Child?

BRAZEN. 'Tis a Project for laying out a thousand Pound.

PLUME. Were it not requisite to project first how to get it in?

BRAZEN. You can't imagine, my Dear, that I want twenty thousand Pound; I have spent twenty times as much in the Service——Now, my Dear, pray advise me, my Head runs much upon Architecture; shall I build a Privateer or a Play-house?

PLUME. An odd Question——A Privateer or a Play-house! 'Twill require some Consideration——Faith, I'm for a Privateer.

BRAZEN. I'm not of your Opinion, my Dear——For in the first place a Privateer may be ill built.

PLUME. And so may a Play-house.

BRAZEN. But a Privateer may be ill mann'd.

PLUME. And so may a Play-house.

BRAZEN. But a Privateer may run upon the Shallows.

PLUME. Not so often as a Play-house.

BRAZEN. But, you know, a Privateer may spring a Leak.

PLUME. And I know that a Play-house may spring a great many.

BRAZEN. But suppose the Privateer come home with a rich Booty, we shou'd never agree about our shares.

PLUME. 'Tis just so in a Play-house——So by my advice, you shall fix upon the Privateer.

BRAZEN. Agreed——But if this twenty-thousand shou'd not be in Specie——

PLUME. What twenty thousand?

BRAZEN. Heark'e——

BRAZEN. Heark'e—— ⟨*Whispers.*⟩

PLUME. Marry'd!

BRAZEN. Presently, we're to meet about half a Mile out of Town at the Water-side——And so forth—— ⟨*Reads.*⟩ For fear I shou'd be known by any of *Worthy*'s Friends, you must give me leave to wear my Mask till after the Ceremony, which will make me ever yours——Look'e there, my dear Dog——

Shows the bottom of the Letter to PLUME.

PLUME. *Melinda!* And by this Light, her own hand!——Once more, if you please, my Dear; her hand exactly!——Just now you say?

BRAZEN. This Minute I must be gone.

PLUME. Have a little Patience, and I'll go with you.

BRAZEN. No, no, I see a Gentleman coming this way that may be inquisitive; 'tis *Worthy*, do you know him?

PLUME. By sight only.

BRAZEN. Have a care, the very Eyes discover Secrets——

Exit.

Enter WORTHY.

WORTHY. To boot, and saddle, Captain, you must mount.

PLUME. Whip and spur, *Worthy*, or you won't mount.

WORTHY. But I shall, *Melinda* and I are agreed, she is gone to visit *Silvia*; we are to mount and follow, and cou'd we carry a Parson with us, who knows what might be done for us both?

PLUME. Don't trouble your Head, *Melinda* has secur'd a Parson already.

WORTHY. Already! Do you know more than I?

PLUME. Yes, I saw it under her hand——*Brazen* and she are to meet half a Mile hence at the Water-side, there to take Boat, I suppose to be ferry'd over to the *Elisian* Fields, if there be any such thing in Matrimony.

WORTHY. I parted with *Melinda* just now, she assur'd me she hated *Brazen*, and that she resolv'd to discard *Lucy* for daring to write Letters to him in her Name.

PLUME. Nay, nay, there's nothing of *Lucy* in this——I tell you I saw *Melinda*'s hand as surely as this is mine.

WORTHY. But I tell you, she's gone this Minute to Justice *Ballance*'s Country House.

PLUME. But I tell you, she's gone this Minute to the Water-side.

Enter a Servant.

Sir. ⟨*To* WORTHY.⟩ Madam *Melinda* has sent word that you need not trouble your self to follow her; because her Journey to Justice *Ballance*'s is put off, and she's gone to take the Air another way.

WORTHY. How! Her Journey put off?

PLUME. That is, her Journey was a put-off to you.

WORTHY. 'Tis plain, plain——But how, where, when is she to meet *Brazen*?

PLUME. Just now, I tell you, half a Mile hence at the Water side.

WORTHY. Up, or down the Water?

PLUME. That I don't know.

WORTHY. I'm glad my Horses are ready——*Jack*, get 'em out.

PLUME. Shall I go with you?

WORTHY. Not an Inch——I shall return presently.

Exit.

PLUME. You'll find me at the Hall, the Justices are sitting by this time, and I must attend them.

Exit.

SCENE V

SCENE, *a Court of Justice*, BALLANCE, SCALE, SCRUPLE, *upon the Bench*. CONSTABLE, KITE, MOB.

KITE *and* CONSTABLE *advance to the Front of the Stage.*

KITE. Pray, who are those honourable Gentlemen upon the Bench?

CONSTABLE. He in the middle is Justice *Ballance*, he on the Right is Justice *Scale*, and he on the Left is Justice *Scruple*, and I am Mr. *Constable*, four very honest Gentlemen.

KITE. O dear, Sir, I'm your most obedient Servant. ⟨*Saluting the Constable.*⟩ I fancy, Sir, that your Employment and mine are much the same, for my Business is to keep People in order, and if they disobey, to knock 'em down; and then we're both Staff-Officers.

CONSTABLE. Nay, I'm a Serjeant my self——Of the Militia——Come, Brother, you shall see me exercise——Suppose this a Musquet now, ⟨*He puts his Staff on his Right Shoulder.*⟩ Now I'm shoulder'd.

KITE. Ay, you're shoulder'd pretty well for a Constable's Staff, but for a Musquet you must put it on t'other Shoulder, my Dear.

CONSTABLE. Adso, that's true,——Come, now give the Word o' Command.

KITE. Silence.

CONSTABLE. Ay, ay, so we will,——We will be silent.

KITE. Silence, you Dog, Silence——

Strikes him over the Head with his Halberd.

CONSTABLE. That's the way to silence a Man with a witness——What d'ye mean, Friend?

KITE. Only to exercise you, Sir.

CONSTABLE. Your Exercise differs so from ours, that we shall ne'er agree about it; if my own Captain had given me such a Rap I had taken the Law of him.

Enter PLUME.

BALLANCE. Captain, you're welcome.

PLUME. Gentlemen, I thank'e.

SCRUPLE. Come, honest Captain, sit by me, ⟨PLUME *ascends, and sits upon the Bench.*⟩ Now produce your Prisoners——Here, that Fellow there,——Set him up——Mr. *Constable*, what have you to say against this Man?

CONSTABLE. I have nothing to say against him, an't please ye.

BALLANCE. No! What made you bring him hither?

CONSTABLE. I don't know, an't please your Worship.

SCRUPLE. Did not the Contents of your Warrant direct you what sort of Men to take up?

CONSTABLE. I can't tell, an't please ye, I can't read.

SCRUPLE. A very pretty Constable truly! I find we have no Business here.

KITE. May it please the Worshipful Bench, I desire to be heard in this Case, as being Counsel for the Queen.

BALLANCE. Come, Serjeant, you shall be heard, since no body else will speak; we won't come here for nothing——

KITE. This Man is but one Man, the Country may spare him, and the Army wants him, besides he's cut out by Nature for a Granadeer, he's five Foot ten Inches high, he shall Box, Wrestle, or dance the *Cheshire* Round with any Man in the County, he gets drunk every Sabbath-Day, and he beats his Wife.

WIFE. You lie, Sirrah, you lie an't please your Worship, he's the best natur'd pains-taking Man in the Parish, witness my five poor Children.

SCRUPLE. A Wife and five Children! you Constable, you Rogue, how durst you Impress a Man that has a Wife and five Children?

SCALE. Discharge him, discharge him.

BALLANCE. Hold, Gentlemen——Hark'e, Friend, how do you maintain your Wife and Children?

PLUME. They live upon Wild Fowl and Venison, Sir, the Husband keeps a Gun, and kills all the Hares and Partridges within five Miles round.

BALLANCE. A Gun! Nay, if he be so good at Gunning he shall have enough on't——He may be of use against the *French*, for he shoots flying to be sure.

SCRUPLE. But his Wife and Children, Mr. *Ballance*.

WIFE. Ay ay, that's the Reason you wou'd send him away——You know I have a Child every year, and you're afraid they should come upon the Parish at last.

PLUME. Look'e there, Gentlemen, the honest Woman has spoke it at once, the Parish had better maintain five Children this Year than six or seven the next; that Fellow upon his high feeding may get you two or three Beggars at a Birth.

WIFE. Look'e, Mr. Captain, the Parish shall get nothing by sending him away, for I won't loose my Teeming Time if there be a Man left in the Parish.

BALLANCE. Send that Woman to the House of Correction——and the Man——

KITE. I'll take care o' him, if you please.

Takes the Man down.

SCALE. Here, you Constable, the next——Set up that black-fac'd Fellow, he has a Gun-powder Look, what can you say against this Man, Constable?

CONSTABLE. Nothing, but that he's a very honest Man.

PLUME. Pray, Gentlemen, let me have one honest Man in my Company for the Novelty's sake.

BALLANCE. What are you, Friend?

MOB. A Collier, I work in the Colepits.

SCRUPLE. Look'e, Gentlemen, this Fellow has a Trade, and the

Act of Parliament here expresses, that we are to impress no Man that has any visible means of a Livelihood.

KITE. May it please your Worships, this Man has no visible means of a Livelihood, for he works under-ground.

PLUME. Well said *Kite*——Besides, the Army wants Miners.

BALLANCE. Right! and had we an Order of Government for't, we cou'd raise you in this and the neighbouring County of *Stafford* five hundred Colliers that wou'd run you under-ground like Moles, and do more Service in a Siege than all the Miners in the Army!

SCRUPLE. Well, Friend, what have you to say for your self?

MOB. I'm Marry'd.

KITE. Lack-a-day, so am I.

MOB. Here's my Wife, poor Woman.

BALLANCE. Are you Marry'd, good Woman?

WOMAN. I'm marry'd in Conscience.

KITE. May it please your Worship, she's with Child in Conscience.

SCALE. Who marry'd you, Mistress?

WOMAN. My Husband——We agreed that I shou'd call him Husband to avoid passing for a Whore, and that he shou'd call me Wife to shun going for a Soldier.

SCRUPLE. A very pretty Couple——Pray, Captain, will you take 'em both——

PLUME. What say you, Mr. *Kite*——Will you take care of the Woman?

KITE. Yes, Sir, she shall go with us to the Sea side, and there if she has a mind to drown her self, we'll take care that no Body shall hinder her.

BALLANCE. Here, Constable, bring in my Man. ⟨*Exit Constable.*⟩ Now Captain, I'll fit you with a Man, such as you ne'er listed in your Life.

Enter CONSTABLE *and* SILVIA.

O my Friend *Pinch*——I'm very glad to see you.

SILVIA. Well, Sir, and what then?

SCALE. What then! Is that your Respect to the Bench?

SILVIA. Sir, I don't care a Farthing for you nor your Bench neither.

SCRUPLE. Look'e, Gentlemen, that's enough, he's a very impudent Fellow, and fit for a Soldier.

SCALE. A notorious Rogue, I say, and very fit for a Soldier.

CONSTABLE. A Whoremaster, I say, and therefore fit to go.

BALLANCE. What think you, Captain?

PLUME. I think he's a very pretty Fellow, and therefore fit to serve.

SILVIA. Me for a Soldier! Send your own lazy lubberly Sons at home, Fellows that hazard their Necks every day in pursuit of a Fox, yet dare not peep abroad to look an Enemy in the Face.

CONSTABLE. May it please your Worships, I have a Woman at the Door to swear a Rape against this Rogue.

SILVIA. Is it your Wife or Daughter, Booby? I ravish'd 'em both yesterday.

BALLANCE. Pray, Captain, read the Articles of War, we'll see him listed immediately.

PLUME *reads Articles of War against Mutiny and Desertion.*

SILVIA. Hold, Sir——Once more, Gentlemen, have a care what you do, for you shall severely smart for any Violence you offer to me, and you, Mr. *Ballance*, I speak to you particularly, you shall heartily repent it.

PLUME. Look'ee, young Spark, say but one Word more and I'll build a Horse for you as high as the Ceiling, and make you ride the most tiresom Journey that ever you made in your Life.

SILVIA. You have made a fine Speech, good Captain *Huffcap*——But you had better be quiet, I shall find a way to cool your Courage.

PLUME. Pray, Gentlemen, don't mind him, he's distracted.

SILVIA. 'Tis false——I'm descended of as good a Family as any in your County, my Father is as good a Man as any upon your Bench, and I am Heir to twelve hundred Pound a Year.

BALLANCE. He's certainly mad,——Pray, Captain, read the Articles of War.

SILVIA. Hold, once more,——Pray, Mr. *Ballance*, to you I speak, suppose I were your Child, wou'd you use me at this rate?

BALLANCE. No Faith, were you mine, I wou'd send you to *Bedlam* first, and into the Army afterwards.

SILVIA. But consider, my Father, Sir, he's as good, as generous, as brave, as just a Man as ever serv'd his Country; I'm his only Child, perhaps the loss of me may break his Heart.

BALLANCE. He's a very great Fool if it does. Captain, if you don't list him this Minute, I'll leave the Court.

PLUME. *Kite*, do you distribute the Levy Money to the Men whilst I read.

KITE. Ay, Sir——Silence, Gentlemen.

PLUME *reads the Articles of War.*

BALLANCE. Very well; now, Captain, let me beg the Favour of you not to discharge this Fellow upon any account whatsoever.——Bring in the rest.

CONSTABLE. There are no more, an't please your Worship.

BALLANCE. No more! there were five two Hours ago.

SILVIA. 'Tis true, Sir, but this Rogue of a Constable let the rest escape for a Bribe of eleven Shillings a Man, because he said that the Act allows him but ten, so the odd Shilling was clear Gains.

ALL JUSTICES. How!

SILVIA. Gentlemen, he offer'd to let me get away for two Guineas, but I had not so much about me.——This is Truth, and I'm ready to swear it.

KITE. And I'll swear it, give me the Book, 'tis for the good of the Service.

MOB. May it please your Worship, I gave him half a Crown to say that I was an honest Man,——and now that your Worships have made me a Rogue, I hope I shall have my Money again.

BALLANCE. 'Tis my Opinion that this Constable be put into the Captain's Hands, and if his Friends don't bring four good Men for his Ransom by to Morrow Night,——Captain, you shall carry him to *Flanders*.

SCALE, SCRUPLE. Agreed, agreed.

PLUME. Mr. *Kite*, take the Constable into Custody.

KITE. Ay, ay; Sir,—— ⟨*To the Constable*⟩ will you please to have your Office taken from you, or will you handsomely lay down your Staff as your Betters have done before you.

The Constable drops his Staff.

BALLANCE. Come, Gentlemen, there needs no great Ceremony in adjourning this Court;——Captain you shall dine with me.

KITE. Come Mr. Militia Serjeant, I shall silence you now I believe, without your taking the Law of me.

Exeunt Omnes.

SCENE VI

SCENE, *changes to the Fields,* BRAZEN *leading in* LUCY *mask'd.*

BRAZEN. The Boat is just below here.

Enter WORTHY *with a Case of Pistols under his Arm, parts* BRAZEN *and* LUCY.

WORTHY. Here, Sir, take your Choice.

Offering the Pistols.

BRAZEN. What! Pistols! are they charg'd, my dear?

WORTHY. With a brace of Bullets each.

BRAZEN. But I'm a Foot Officer, my dear, and never use Pistols, the Sword is my way, and I won't be put out of my Road to please any Man.

WORTHY. Nor I neither, so have at you.

Cocks one Pistol.

BRAZEN. Look'e, my dear, I do not care for Pistols;——pray oblige me and let us have a bout at Sharps, dam't there's no parrying these Bullets.

WORTHY. Sir, if you han't your Belly full of these, the Swords shall come in for Second Course.

BRAZEN. Why then Fire and Fury! I have eaten Smoak from the Mouth of a Cannon; Sir, don't think I fear Powder, for I live upon't; let me see, ⟨*Takes a Pistol*⟩ and now, Sir, how many paces distant shall we fire?

WORTHY. Fire you when you please, I'll reserve my shot till I be sure of you.

BRAZEN. Come, where's your Cloak?

WORTHY. Cloak! what d'ye mean?

BRAZEN. To fight upon, I always fight upon a Cloak, 'tis our way abroad.

LUCIA. Come, Gentlemen, I'll end the Strife.

Pulls off her Mask.

WORTHY. *Lucy!* take her.

BRAZEN. The Devil take me if I do——Huzza, ⟨*Fires his Pistol*⟩ d'ye hear, d'ye hear, you plaguy Harrydan, how those

Bullets whistle, suppose they had been lodg'd in my Gizzard now?——

LUCIA. Pray, Sir, pardon me.

BRAZEN. I can't tell, Child, till I know whether my Money be safe; 〈*Searching his Pockets.*〉 Yes, yes, I do pardon you,—— but if I had you in the *Rose* Tavern, *Covent Garden*, with three or four hearty Rakes, and three or four smart Napkins, I would tell you another Story, my dear.

Exit.

WORTHY. And was *Melinda* privy to this?

LUCIA. No, Sir, she wrote her Name upon a piece of Paper at the Fortune-tellers last Night, which I put in my Pocket, and so writ above it to the Captain.

WORTHY. And how came *Melinda*'s Journey put off?

LUCIA. At the Towns end she met Mr. *Ballance*'s Steward, who told her that Mrs. *Silvia* was gone from her Father's, and no body could tell whither.

WORTHY. *Silvia* gone from her Father's! this will be News to *Plume*. Go home, and tell your Lady how near I was being shot for her.

Exeunt.

Enter BALLANCE *with a Napkin in his Hand as risen from Dinner, talking with his Steward.*

STEWARD. We did not miss her till the Evening, Sir, and then searching for her in the Chamber that was my young Master's, we found her Cloaths there, but the Suit that your Son left in the Press when he went to *London*, was gone.

BALLANCE. The white, trimm'd with Silver!

STEWARD. The same.

BALLANCE. You han't told that Circumstance to any body.

STEWARD. To none but your Worship.

BALLANCE. And be sure you don't. Go into the Dining Room, and tell Captain *Plume* that I beg to speak with him.

STEWARD. I shall.

BALLANCE. Was ever man so impos'd upon? I had her Promise indeed that she shou'd never dispose of herself without my Consent.——I have consented with a Witness, given her away as my Act and Deed; and this, I warrant, the Captain thinks will pass; no, I shall never pardon him the Villany, first of robbing me of my Daughter, and then the mean Opinion he must have of me to think that I cou'd be so wretchedly imposed upon; her extravagant Passion might encourage her in the Attempt, but the Contrivance must be his——I'll know the Truth presently.

Enter PLUME.

Pray, Captain, what have you done with your young Gentleman Souldier?

PLUME. He's at my Quarters, I suppose, with the rest of my Men.

BALLANCE. Does he keep Company with the Common Souldiers?

PLUME. No, he's generally with me.

BALLANCE. He lies with you, I presume.

PLUME. No, Faith,——I offer'd him part of my Bed, but the young Rogue fell in love with *Rose*, and has layn with her, I think, since he came to Town.

BALLANCE. So that between you both, *Rose* has been finely manag'd.

PLUME. Upon my Honour, Sir, she had no harm from me.

BALLANCE. All's safe, I find——Now Captain, you must know that the young Fellow's Impudence in Court was well grounded; he said that I should heartily repent his being listed, and I do from my Soul.

PLUME. Ay! for what reason?

BALLANCE. Because he is no less than what he said he was, born of as good a Family as any in this County, and is Heir to twelve hundred pound a Year.

PLUME. I'm very glad to hear it, for I wanted but a Man of that Quality to make my Company a perfect Representative of the whole Commons of *England*.

BALLANCE. Won't you discharge him?

PLUME. Not under a hundred Pound Sterling.

BALLANCE. You shall have it, for his Father is my intimate Friend.

PLUME. Then you shall have him for nothing.

BALLANCE. Nay, Sir, you shall have your Price.

PLUME. Not a Penny, Sir, I value an Obligation to you much above a hundred Pound.

BALLANCE. Perhaps, Sir, you shan't repent your Generosity. Will you please to write his Discharge in my Pocket Book. ⟨*Gives his Book.*⟩ In the mean time we'll send for the Gentleman. Who waits there?

Enter Servant.

Go to the Captain's Lodgings, and inquire for Mr. *Wilfull*, tell him his Captain wants him here immediately.

SERVANT. Sir, the Gentleman's below at the Door enquiring for the Captain.

PLUME. Bid him come up——here's the Discharge, Sir.——

BALLANCE. Sir, I thank you—— ⟨*Aside.*⟩ 'tis plain he had no hand in't.

Enter SILVIA.

SILVIA. I think, Captain, you might have us'd me better, than to leave me yonder among your swearing, drunken Crew; and you, Mr. Justice, might have been so civil as to have invited me to Dinner, for I have eaten with as good a Man as your Worship.

PLUME. Sir, you must charge our want of Respect upon our Ignorance of your Quality——but now you're at Liberty——I have discharged you.

SILVIA. Discharg'd me!

BALLANCE. Yes, Sir, and you must once more go home to your Father.

SILVIA. My Father! then I'm discovered——O, Sir, ⟨*Kneeling.*⟩ I expect no Pardon.

BALLANCE. Pardon! no, no, Child; your Crime shall be your Punishment; here, Captain, I deliver her over to the conjugal Power for her Chastisement; since she will be a Wife, be you a Husband, a very Husband: when she tells you of her Love, upbraid her with her Folly, be modishly ungrateful, because she has been unfashionably kind; and use her worse than you wou'd any Body else, because you can't use her so well as she deserves.

PLUME. And are you *Silvia* in good earnest?

SILVIA. Earnest! I have gone too far to make it a Jest, Sir.

PLUME. And do you give her to me in good earnest?

BALLANCE. If you please to take her, Sir.

PLUME. Why then I have sav'd my Legs and Arms, and lost my Liberty, secure from Wounds I'm prepar'd for the Gout, farewel Subsistence, and welcome Taxes——Sir, my Liberty and hopes of being a General are much dearer to me than your twelve hundred Pound a Year, but to your Love, Madam, I resign my Freedom, and to your Beauty, my Ambition; greater in obeying at your Feet, than Commanding at the Head of an Army.

Enter WORTHY.

WORTHY. I'm sorry to hear, Mr. *Ballance*, that your Daughter is lost.

BALLANCE. So am not I, Sir, since an honest Gentleman has found her.

Enter MELINDA.

MELINDA. Pray, Mr. *Ballance*, what's become of my Cousin *Silvia*?

BALLANCE. Your Cousin *Silvia* is talking yonder with your Cousin *Plume*.

MELINDA *and* WORTHY. How!

SILVIA. Do you think it strange, Cousin, that a Woman should change? But, I hope, you'll excuse a Change that has proceeded from Constancy, I alter'd my Outside, because I was the same within, and only laid by the Woman to make sure of my Man, that's my History.

MELINDA. Your History is a little romantick, Cousin, but since Success has crown'd your Adventures you will have the World o' your side, and I shall be willing to go with the Tide, provided you pardon an Injury I offer'd you in the Letter to your Father.

PLUME. That Injury, Madam, was done to me, and the Reparation I expect shall be made to my Friend, make Mr. *Worthy* happy, and I shall be satisfy'd.

MELINDA. A good Example, Sir, will go a great way——when my Cousin is pleas'd to surrender, 'tis probable, I shan't hold out much longer.

Enter BRAZEN.

BRAZEN. Gentlemen, I am yours, Madam, I am not yours.

MELINDA. I'm glad on't, Sir.

BRAZEN. So am I——you have got a pretty House here, Mr. *Laconick*.

BALLANCE. 'Tis time to right all Mistakes——my Name, Sir, is *Ballance*.

BRAZEN. *Ballance!* Sir, I'm your most obedient.——I know your whole Generation,——had not you an Unkle that was Governour of the *Leeward* Islands some Years ago?

BALLANCE. Did you know him?

BRAZEN. Intimately, Sir, he play'd at Billiards to a miracle; you had a Brother too, that was Captain of a Fireship——poor *Dick*, he had the most engaging way with him——of making Punch,——and then his Cabbin was so neat——but his Boy *Jack* was the most comical Bastard, ha, ha, ha, a pickled Dog, I shall never forget him.

PLUME. Well, Captain, are you fix'd in your Project yet, are you still for the Privateer?

BRAZEN. No, no, I had enough of a Privateer just now, I had like to have been pick'd up by a Cruiser under false Colours, and a *French* Pickaroon for ought I know.

PLUME. But have you got your Recruits, my Dear?

BRAZEN. Not a Stick, my Dear.

PLUME. Probably I shall furnish you.

Enter ROSE *and* BULLOCK.

ROSE. Captain, Captain, I have got loose once more, and have persuaded my Sweetheart *Cartwheel*, to go with us, but you must promise not to part with me again.

SILVIA. I find Mrs. *Rose* has not been pleas'd with her Bedfellow.

ROSE. Bedfellow! I don't know whether I had a Bedfellow or not.

SILVIA. Don't be in a Passion, Child, I was as little pleas'd with your Company as you cou'd be with mine.

BULLOCK. Pray, Sir, dunna be offended at my Sister, she's some-thing underbred——but if you please I'll lye with you in her stead.

PLUME. I have promised, Madam, to provide for this Girl; now will you be pleas'd to let her wait upon you, or shall I take care of her.

SILVIA. She shall be my Charge, Sir, you may find it Business enough to take care of me.

BULLOCK. Ay, and of me, Captain, for wauns if ever you lift your Hand against me, I'll desert.

PLUME. Captain *Brazen* shall take care o' that——My Dear, instead of the twenty thousand Pound you talk'd of, you shall have the twenty brave Recruits that I have rais'd, at the rate they cost me——my Commission I lay down to be taken up by some braver Fellow, that has more Merit, and less good Fortune, whilst I endeavour by the Example of this worthy Gentleman to serve my Queen and Country at home.

With some Regret I quit the active Field,
Where Glory full reward for Life does yield;
But the Recruiting Trade with all its train,
Of lasting Plague, Fatigue, and endless Pain,
I gladly quit, with my fair Spouse to stay,
And raise Recruits the Matrimonial Way.

EPILOGUE

All Ladies and Gentlemen, that are willing to see the Comedy call'd the *Recruiting Officer*, let them repair to morrow Night by six a Clock to the Sign of the *Theatre Royal* in *Drury Lane*, and they shall be kindly entertain'd——

We scorn the vulgar Ways to bid you come,
Whole Europe *now obeys the Call of Drum.*
The Soldier, not the Poet, here appears,
And beats up for a Corps *of Volunteers:*
He finds that Musick chiefly do's delight ye,
And therefore chuses Musick to invite ye.

Beat the Granadeer-March——Row, row, tow——Gentlemen, this Piece of Musick, call'd an *Overture to a Battel,* was compos'd by a famous *Italian* Master, and was perform'd with wonderful Success, at the great *Opera*'s of *Vigo, Schellenberg,* and *Blenheim*; it came off with the Applause of all *Europe*, excepting *France*; the *French* found it a little too rough for their *Delicatesse.*

Some that have acted on those glorious Stages,
Are her to witness to succeeding Ages,
That no Musick like the Granadeer's engages.

Ladies, we must own that this Musick of ours is not altogether so soft as *Bononcini*'s, yet we dare affirm, that it has laid more People asleep than all the *Camilla*'s in the World; and you'll condescend to own, that it keeps one awake, better than any *Opera* that ever was acted.

The Granadeer March seems to be a Composure excellently adapted to the Genius of the *English*; for no Musick was ever follow'd so far by us, nor with so much Alacrity; and with all Deference to the present Subscription, we must say that the Granadeer March has been subscrib'd for by the whole Grand Alliance; and we presume to inform the Ladies, that it always has the Pre-eminence abroad, and is constantly heard by the tallest, handsomest Men in the whole Army. In short, to gratifie the present Taste, our

Author is now adapting some Words to the Granadeer-March, which he intends to have perform'd to Morrow, if the Lady who is to sing it shou'd not happen to be sick.

This he concludes to be the surest way
To draw you hither, for you'll all obey
Soft Musick's Call, tho' you shou'd damn his Play.

TEXTUAL NOTES

SIGLA

A = First edition, copy text
B = Second edition, 'corrected'
C = Third edition, 'corrected'

TITLE PAGE

is] A B; was C
DRURY] A C; DRYRY B
Captique dolis] A (errata) B C; Captique Aeolis A

THE EPISTLE DEDICATORY

Dedication round] A; Round B C
6 leave] A; Leave B C
8 fortune] A; Fortune B C
10 *Salop*;] A; *Salop*, B C
20 *Wrekin*] A (errata) B C; Rekin A
22 rise] A B; Rise C
24 expence] A; Expence B C
24 Country Gentlemen] A; Country-Gentlemen B C
28 *puris Naturalibus*] A B; Puris Naturalibus C
36 lyes A]; lies B C
37 him for] A; him, for B C
53 Recruiting Officer] A; *Recruiting Officer* B C
54 Spoke] A B; Spake C
61 *Friends round*] A; *Friends, round* B C
62 *Wrekin*] A (errata) B C; *Rekin* A
69 Obliged] A; obliged B C
70 Obedient] A; obedient B C

THE PROLOGUE

6 *Deserter*, lay] A; Deserter lay B C
7 had] A C; hath B
14 Young Aspiring] A; young aspiring B C
17 *Fair* Hellen] A; *fair* Hellen B C
18 One Hellen] A; *One* Hellen B C
27 many Hellens] A; Many Hellens B C

DRAMATIS PERSONAE

2 Mr. Phillips] A B; Mr. Philips C
8 Countrey] A; Country B C
9 Recruits,] A; Recruits. B C
15 Countrey] A; Country B C

ACT 1. SCENE 1.

1 Soldiers] A C; Souldiers B
2 King, if] A; King: If B C
4 Parents;] A; Parents: B C
5 Wife, let] A; Wife: Let B C
5 Noble] A B; noble C
6 *Raven*] A; Raven B C
7 Relief and] A C; Relief, and B
7 Entertainment.—] A; Entertainment—B C
10 Soldiers] A C; Souldiers B
11 Pray Gentlemen observe] A; Pray, gentlemen, observe B C
14 Fortune] A; fortune B C
15 (*To one of the Mob*)] A; B and C omit
15 Will] A; will B C
19 you.] A; you? B C
20 in it, no] A; in it? no B C

20 Gun-powder-plot] A; Gun-powder Plot B C
23 plaguely] A; plaguily B C
24 Brimstone; pray] A; Brimstone. Pray B C
27 KITE] B C; *Serj* A
27 *The Crown, or the Bed of Honour*] A; The Crown, or the Bed of Honour B C
28 *Bed of Honour?*] A; Bed of Honour B C
29 KITE] B C; *Serj* A
29 O,] A; O! B C
29 Bed, bigger] A; Bed! bigger B C
30 *Ware*, ten] A; *Ware*—ten B C
30 lie] A C; lye B
32 lie] A C; lye B
34 *Bed of Honour?*] A; Bed of Honour? B C
35 KITE] B C; *Serj* A
35 Ay] A; ay B C
35 sound that] A; sound, that B C
35 wake] A B; awake C
37 KITE] B C; *Serj* A
37 Then I find Brother] A; then, I find, Brother B C
38 Hold] A; hold B C
38 there Friend] A; there, Friend B C
38 I'm] A; I am B C
39 of, as yet] A; of yet B C
39 Lookye Serjeant] A; Look'ee Serjeant B C
39 coaxing] A; Coaxing B C
39 wheedling] A; Wheedling B C
40 d'ye'see;] A; d'ye see—B C
40 if] A; If B C
40 why 'tis] A; why, 'tis B C
41 Therefore] A; therefore B C
42 an't] A; am not B C
42 coaxing] A; Coaxing B C
43 Faith] A; faith B C
47 Spirit, but] A; Spirit; but B C
47 base;] A; base: B C
48 tho'] A; Tho' B C
48 a better built Man] A; a Man better built B C
49 : How] A; ; how
49 treads, he] A; treads! He B C
49 Castle! But] A; castle; but B C
52 he] A; He B C
53 Pardon Sir] A; Pardon, Sir B C
55 hand then, and] A; Hand then; and B C
55 now Gentlemen] A; now, Gentlemen B C
56 say but] A; say, but B C
57 Quarters,' tis] A; Quarters—'Tis
58 Drink;] A; Drink—B C
60 Health.] A; Health? B C
64 Huzza.] A; Huzza! B C
65 *Exeunt, Drum*] A; *Exit Drum* B C
65 *the Granadeer-March*] A; *a Granadeers March* B C
66 Drum] A C; Brum B
67 Shout it] A; Shout, it B C
67 Let me see—(*Looks on his Watch*) Four a Clock—at ten] A; Let me see—Four a Clock—(Looking on his Watch.) At Ten B C
68 Yesterday] A; yesterday B C
69 hundred and twenty] A; Hundred and Twenty B C
69 thirty] A; Thirty B C
70 riding] A; Riding B C
70 Hours, is] A; Hours is B C
70 Fatigue] A; fatigue B C
72 Welcome] A; Wellcome B C
72 Captain, from] A; Captain: From B C
73 Captain you are] A; Captain, you're B C
73 welcome] A; wellcome B C
74 *Kite*,] A; *Kite*: B C
75 What] A; what B C
80 Gypsies] A; *Gipsies* B C
82 Wer't] A; wer't B C
84 Why Sir?] A; Why, Sir? B C
85 Body] A; body B C
86 say, this] A; say this B C
90 Umh–] A; Hum!
92 News] A; news B C
97 here that] A; here, that B C

99 for last] A; for the last B C
99 Country; you] A; Country: You B C
100 *Castle*] A; Castle? B C
102 Bed Yesterday] A; bed yesterday B C
103 Father] A; father B C
104 Humph—And] A; And B C
106 If they] B C; If she A
106 us, she] A; us; she B C
107 Occasion, but] A; occasion. But B C
109 I'm] A; I am B C
112 Muster-Roll] A; Muster Roll B C
112 *Draws out the Muster-Roll*] A; *Draws it out* B C
113 *Snickereyes*] A; *Snikereyes* B C
114 Guzzle, the] A; Guzzle the B C
115 Woman at] A; Woman, at B C
116 in *Hull*] A; at *Hull* B C
116 Madamoseille] A; Madamoiselle B C
117 Van-Bottomflat] A; Van-bottom-flat B C
117 *Okam*] A; Oakam B C
121 Company, you] A; Company—You B
121 five] A; Five B C
122 Dozen, *Kite*—Is] A; Dozen,—*Kite*—Is B C
122 Boy or] A; Boy, or
125 mine; enter] A; mine: Enter B C
126 *Furlow*] A; Furlow B C
126 Subsistence, and] A; Subsistance; and B C
129 Use] A; use B C
131 Sir;] A; Sir, B C
131 Country, for] A; Country for B C
132 famous] A; faithful B C
133 Secret for] A; Secret, for B C
134 trusty] A; faithful B C
135 confided] A; trusted B C
135 him:] A; him. B C
137 Friend, Mr.] A; Friend Mr. B C
139 present. (*Exit*)] B C; present (*Exit*) A
139 'Tis] B C; 'tis A
141 What! Arms] A; What Arms B C
141 *Worthy*!] A; *Worthy*? B C
142 open when] A; open, when B C
143 Ears I] A; Ears, I B C
143 believe.] A; believe: B C
143 melancholy] A; melancholly B C
145 *Spleen . . . Blow*] A; B prints in Roman, and inserts a comma after 'thee' in 2nd line
147 My] A; my B C
147 welcome, safe] A; welcome. Safe B C
150 Nose—Then] A; Nose; then B
151 inside] A; Inside B C
155 dead] A B; Dead C
158 Then, you] A; Then you B C
162 dwindled] A; dwindl'd B C
164 pray, What] A; pray, what B C
166 hands Brother] A; Hands, Brother B C
166 you] A; thou B C
166 that—Behold] A; that, behold B C
170 Woman, 'sdeath,] A; Woman! S'death! B C
171 melancholy] A B; melancholly C
172 Pickle?] A; Condition? B C
172 Pray, who] A; Pray who B C
173 miraculous] A; wonderful B C
174 ten Year's] A; Ten Years B C
176 Pho—Is] A; Pho! Is B C
178 pities—But] A; pities; But B C
181 Impossible] A; That's impossible B C
182 Year's] A; Years B C
183 *Melinda*?] A C; *Melinda*! B
184 Twelve-month] A; Twelvemonth B C
188 to't] A; to'it B C
189 consider; when] A; consider—When B C
192 *Richly* her] A; *Richly*, her B C
192 *Flintshire* dies] A; Flintshire, dies B C
193 her at] A; her, at B C
193 time twenty] A; Time, twenty B C
193 Pound]; Pounds B C

194 Devil, what] A; Devil! What B C
195 now, *Worthy*] A; now,—*Worthy* B C
195 *Worthy*, your Blockade] A; *Worthy*, Blockade B C
196 —After] A;—after B C
197 thought] A; Thought B C
197 Famine—You] A; Famine, you B C
198 redoubled] A; redoubl'd B C
201 despairing] A C; dispairing B
205 So, as] A; So as B C
209 all— A; all.—B C
211 Humility—Wou'd] A; Humility: Wou'd B C
213 self—Let] A; self.—Let B C
213 see—The] A; see, the B C
215 Neighbourhood to] A; Neighbourhood, to B C
216 Child. Suppose] A; Child.—Suppose B C
217 out? Or] A; out; or B C
218 her, with] A; her with B C
218 Ugliest.] A; ugliest. B C
219 confess,—But] A; confess; but B C
220 precise, dull] A; precise dull B C
222 No] A; no B C
225 Good-will] A; Good Will B C
226 Blood—Witness] A; Blood, witness B C
227 Molly] A; *Molley* B C
227 *Castle*—] A; Castle,—B C
227 There] A; there B C
229 hope] A; hope, B C
229 of't] A; of it B C
230 Sir,] A; Sir! B C
232 my own quite] A; mine quit B mine quite C
232 Head:] A; Head. B C
234 Preliminaries; but] A; Preliminaries, but B C
236 Wedding—We] A; Wedding; we B C
236 agree, she] A; agree. She B C
237 Maidenhead] A; Maiden-head B C
239 Conditions.] A; Conditions? B C
240 Conditions] A; Conditions B C
240 all, if] A; all—If B C
241 I'm] A; I am B C
242 till] A; 'till B C
243 Hour—Suppose] A; Hour. Suppose B C
244 Leg? Such] A; Leg—such B C
244 before-hand; if] A; before hand—if B; beforehand—if C
248 Say, That] A; say, that B C
250 If] A; if B C
252 Ground–] A; Ground.—B C
252 *Silvia*] A C; *Sylvia* B
253 Disposition; there's] A; Disposition—There's B C
254 foil] A; Foil B C
254 her–] A; her.—B C
257 General] A C; general B
258 reason; for] A; Reason—For B
259 coquets] A B; Coquets C
260 I lay] A B; I'll lay C
260 Pound she] A; Pound, she B C
260 love] A; Love B C
263 Lookye] A; look'e B C
263 her, and] A; her and B C
264 Faith;] A; Faith, B C
265 give a Fig for] A; value B C
268 You] B C; Your A
270 *Molly*] A; *Molley* B C
270 My] A; my B C
271 Oho,] A; O, ho! B C
271 well—] A; well! B C
272 may,—for] A; may—For B C
273 Hour,—but] A; Hour—But B; hour—But C
273 a saying] A; saying B C
274 *Molly*—My] A; Molly—my B C
274 Wife, I] A; wife I B C
274 mean. But] A; mean—But B C
275 think Sir] A; think, Sir B C
276 how?] A; how! B C
277 Livery had] A; Livery, had B C
278 Baby Cloaths] A; Baby-cloaths B C
279 Wonder, cou'd] A; wonder cou'd B C

280 s.d. *Whispers* Plume] A; *Whispers* B C
281 Creature.] A; Creature! B C
282 Impossible.] A; Impossible! B C
283 be] A; are B C
283 Guinea's] A; Guineas B C
283 part] A; Part B C
284 wife's] A; wifes B C
284 Portion:] A; Portion. B C
284 Nay farther] A; Nay, farther B C
285 that] A; B C omit
286 God-mother] A; Godmother B C
286 Footman, as] A; Footman as B C
288 went; and] A; went and B; went, and C
289 News, and] A; News; and B C
290 you, That] A; you, that B C
291 Country, wou'd] A; Country wou'd B; Country would C
292 *Worthy*—] A; *Worthy*,— B C
293 noble and generous] A; B C omit and and substitute a comma
293 Manly] A; manly B C
294 Friendship,] A; Friendship; B C
294 show] A; shew B C
295 Prerogative that] A; Prerogative —That B C
295 way, without] A; way without B C
295 Fits, and] A; Fits and B C
298 Come *Worthy*] A; Come, *Worthy* B C
299 quarter] A; Quarter B C
302 welcome] A; Welcome B C
303 then—] A; then,—B C
304 her, That I] A; her I B C
305 on her] A; upon her B C
310 place] A; Place B C
311 But] A; but B C

ACT I. SCENE II

1 Cosin] A; Cousin B C
3 living,] A; living; B C
5 Spleen, and] A; Spleen,—B C
6 Then the] A; Then, the B C
7 Madam,] A; Madam! B C
10 in it;] A; in't! B C
10 Lady the] A B; Lady, the C
10 nice] A; Nice B C
11 Constitution, no] A; Constitution —No B C
11 Air I] A; Air, I B C
11 Year; Change] A; Year. Change B C
12 Air I] A; Air, I B C
13 Cosin] A; Cousin B C
14 airs in conversation . . . impudent airs] A: B C omit
17 Pshaw—I] A; Psha! I B C
20 Pray Cosin,] A; Pray, Cousin, B C
20 Taste] A; taste B C
21 You] A; you B C
21 may] A; might B C
21 me I might] A; me, I may B C
21 Air; A; Air: B C
21 prithee, my] A; prithee my B C
22 Airs] A; an Air B C
22 me, your] A; me. Your B C
23 time when] A; time, when B C
25 Noses drop] A; fingers ake B C
26 Boarding-School] A C; Boarding School B
27 Cosin] A; Cousin B C
28 a Horse] A; an horse B C
30 troubled] A; troubl'd B C
30 Cholick] A; Collick
31 Vapours, I] A; Vapours; I B C
31 Salt] A; Salts B C
32 gallop] A; Gallop B C
33 Hunting Horn] A; Hunting-horn B C
34 Fiddle:] A; Fiddle. B C
34 Father but] A; Father, but B C
34 drink and] A; drink, and B C
35 I'm sure] A; I am sure B C
36 Tryal] A; Trial B C
37 You're] You're are] A; You are B C
37 to't;] A; to't, B C
37 I'm] A; I am B C
37 told, your] A; told your B C

41 You're] A; Your are B; You are C
41 Cosin] A; Cousin B C
42 *And there's a Pleasure sure, in being mad, Which none but Madmen know*] A; B C set in roman, as prose, omitting *sure*,
44 Romantick] A; romantick B C
44 *Quixote*, hast] A; *Quixote*—Haste B; *Quixote*—Hast C
45 imagine that] A; imagine, that B C
45 Officer that] A; Officer, that B C
45 over] A; o'er B; o're C
47 Justice in] A; Justice, in B C
47 corner] A; Part B C
47 World? A; World. B C
48 Pshaw!] A; Psha! B C
48 Thoughts? A; Thoughts; B C
49 shows] A; shews B C
50 dull, sleepy] A; dull sleepy B C
50 best;] A; best, B C
51 Vertues, nor] A; Virtues; nor B C
53 Sex.] A; Sex—B C
54 I'm] A; I am B C
57 handsomly] A; handsomely B C
58 hadst] A; had'st B C
59 *Christendom*] A; Christendom B C
60 endeavour] A; have endeavour'd B C
61 thoroughly] A; thoroughly, B C
62 Amours. But] A; Amours; but B C
65 Vapours.] A; Vapours! B C
67 inhumanely, he's] A; inhumanly. He's B C
68 and beside that he's] A; And besides that, he's B C
69 Friend; and] A; Friend, and B C
73 Captain; for] A; Captain, for B C
75 Oh! Madam—] A; O, Madam! B C
76 Pound] A; Pounds B C
78 incourage] A; encourage B C
78 loose and] A; loose, and B C
82 Madam—for] A; Madam, for B C
82 You're] A; you are B C
84 Plainness] A; plainness B C
85 Ladyship as] A; Ladyship's as B C
86 assur'd] A; sure B C
86 shou'd] A B; wou'd C
87 Rakely] A; rakhelly B; rakehelly C
87 Officer as] A C; Officer, as B
88 Madam—You're] A; Madam, you're B C
91 Madam—I] A; Madam, I B C
93 this, the] A; this the B C
95 I'm easily advis'd] A; I am easily persuaded B C
95 Inclinations—So Madam] A; Inclinations, so, Madam B C
99 you not] A; not you B C
99 swells] A; swell'd B C
100 Fellow?] A; Fellow. B C
102 Madam—I] A; Madam; I B C
104 it; let] A; it—Let B C
105 Hold] A; hold B C
106 Madam—] A; Madam. B C
109 him; send] A; him, send B C
111 Madam—] A; Madam. B C
112 shall] A; shou'd B C
113 s.d. *exeunt severally*] A; B C omit *severally*

ACT II. SCENE I

2 Men; I] A; Men. I B C
2 remember, that] A; remember that B C
3 Blood nor Wounds but] A; Blood, no Wounds B C
3 Officers Mouths, nothing] A; Officer's Mouths; Nothing B C
4 News Papers] A; News-Papers B C
5 reading, our] A; Reading—Our B C
5 Armies] A; Army B C
5 Bars] A; Barrs B C
6 Enemy,] A; Enemy; B C
7 Standards] A C; Standarts B
7 Prisoners; odsmylife] A; Prisoners—Ad's my Life B C
8 Mareschal] A; Marshal B C

9 Soldier.] A; Souldier.—B; Soldier.—C
10 Pray, Mr] A; Pray Mr B C
10 does] A C; do's B
11 Ah! Captain,] A; Ah, Captain! B C
11 Mareschal] A; Marshal B C
13 Battel] A; Battle B C
13 *Hochstet*] A; *Hockstat* B C
17 General] B C; Generals A
17 so,] A; so; B C
18 pleases to] A; pleases but to B C
18 again—]; agen. B C
19 does] A; do's B C
20 Captain—You're] A; Captain, you are B C
21 War, Victory B C]; War, War A
26 How Sir!] A; How, Sir! B C
27 she is] A; she's B C
30 now by] A; now, by B C
31 then,] A; then; B C
32 old plain Country A]; old Country B C
37 breaks; the] A; breaks, the B C
37 Favours, Sir] A C; Favours Sir B
39 Pho!] A; Pho, B C
40 cou'd] A; could B C
42 know;] A; know: B C
42 than] A C; then B
43 Camp: But] A; Camp, but B C
45 *Silvia.*] A; *Silvia*! B C
48 *Germany*] A; *Germany*, B C
49 go read] A; go and read B C
49 Letters and] A; Letters, and B C
51 You're] A; you are B C
52 *PLUME* Blessings . . . *SILVIA* . . . fair Quarter. PLUME . . . at your Feet] A; these three speeches are replaced as follows in B C

PLUME You are indebted to me a Welcome, Madam, since the hopes of receiving it from this fair Hand, was the Principal Cause of my seeing *England*.

SILVIA I have often heard that Soldiers were sincere, shall I venture to believe Publick Report?

PLUME You may, when 'tis back'd by private Insurance; for I swear, Madam, by the Honour of my Profession, that whatever Dangers I went upon, it was with the hope of making my self more worthy of your Esteem, and if ever I had thoughts of preserving my Life, 'twas for the Pleasure of dying at your Feet

die] A C; dye B

first let me desire you to make your Will, perhaps you'll leave me something] A; you know, Sir, there is a certain Will and Testament to be made beforehand B C

Gives her a Parchment] A; this stage direction is omitted in B C

SILVIA opens the Will, and reads] A; this stage direction is placed after Mrs *Silvia Ballance* in B C, the commas after Will being omitted.

64 *Ballance*—] A; *Ballance*, B C
64 handsome and] A; handsome, and B C
65 Compliment,] A; Complement; B C
65 you I] A; you, I B C
66 Knowledge] A; knowledge B C
67 Legacy; but] A; Legacy: But B C
69 *Castle*] A; Castle B C
70 home;] A; home, B C
71 my] A; My B C
74 Necessity, that] A; Necessity.—That B C
74 all Madam,—] A; all, Madam.—B C
74 my] A; My B C
74 No, no.] A; No, no, no. B C
75 *Enter Servant*] A; *Enter a Servant* B C
78 Pardon that] A; Pardon, that B C
79 it;] A; it, B C
80 afflicted;] A; afflicted: B C
81 assur'd that] A; assur'd, that B C
83 he] B C; she A

84 pressing, that] A; pressing that B C
85 do] A; endanger B C

ACT II. SCENE II.

SCENE changes to another Apartment] A; SCENE, *Another Appartment* B C
1 hope] A; hopes B C
1 Sir;] A; Sir, B C
3 reason] A; Reason B C
3 it. Dr.] A; it; Doctor B C
4 hands] A; Hands B C
5 Son—] A; Son.—B C
7 I'm] A; I am B C
8 mine.] A; mine; B C
9 Hopes] A; hopes B C
10 Thoughts and] A; Thoughts, and B C
11 desire] A; Desire B C
14 which three or four Years hence will amount to twelve hundred Pound *per Annum*; this] A; which you know is about twelve hundred Pounds a Year; This B C
16 Quality and] A; Quality, and B C
16 Title, you] A; Title; you
16 Value] A; value B C
17 Terms think] A; Terms, think B C
21 Family,] A; Family; B C
22 Pound, indeed] A; Pounds indeed B C
22 hands] A; Hands B C
23 but odsmylife,] A; but,—od's my Life,
23 Pound] A; Pounds B C
24 ruine] A; ruin B C
24 Brain.] A; Brain: B C
25 Pound] A; Pounds B C
27 That] A; that B C
27 mad, for you] A; mad: For you B; mad: Foryou C
28 know that] A; know, that B C
28 Aversion] A C; aversion B
29 standing; then] A; standing. Then B C
30 Builder by] A; Builder, by B C
30 Art transform] A; Art, transform B C
31 Portals] A; Portalls B C
32 Beasts, Gods and Devils] A; Beasts and Devils B C
34 *Firma*] A; *firma* B C
35 *Chelsea* or] A; Chelsea, or B C
35 *Twitnam*] A; *Twitnenham* B C
35 Grass-plats] A; Grass-Plats B
35 Gravel-walks] A; Gravel-Walks B C
37 here's] A; Here is B C
37 one below with a Letter] A; one with a Letter below B C
38 hands] A; Hands B C
39 show] A; shew B C
Exit] A; *Ex* B C
41 exactly—] A; exactly.—B C
41 Ah! poor] A; ah poor B C
42 Brother;] A; Brother! B C
42 Ah! poor] A; Ah poor B C
42 Sister—] A; Sister! B C
42 ways, I'll] A; ways; I'll B C
43 try again, follow] A; try it again, —Follow B C
44 Heart, or] A; Heart; or B C
44 Commands and] A; Commands, and B C
44 own,] A; own; B C
44 worse—] A; worse. B C
45 take thus—] A; take it thus? B C
46 Fellow and] A C; Fellow, and B
46 Pad,—or] A; Pad; or B C
48 *To the Servant who goes out.*] A; *To a Servant, who goes out.* B C
49 *Silvia.*] *Silvia*, A; Ho *Silvia*! B C
52 young that] A; young, that B C
57 Never, that] A; Never that B C
58 Then *Silvia*] A; Then, *Silvia* B C
61 command—I] A; command; I B C
63 Advice proceed] A; Advice, Sir, proceed B C
67 shall] A; will B C
67 days] A; Days B C
68 Reasons—] A; Reasons.—B C
74 promise, That I] A; promise I B C

71 will never] A; never will B C
72 Consent;] A; Consent, B C
75 so *Silvia*] A; so, *Silvia* B C
76 *Door and*] A; *Door, and* B C
81 *Friendship and*] A; *Friendship, and* B C
82 *Family oblige*] A; *Family, oblige* B C
83 it; the] A; it: The B C
83 *Cosin*] A; *Cousin* B C
83 SILVIA] Silvia, A; Silvia; B C
85 *Cosin*] A; *Cousin* B C
85 *Country is*] A; *Country, is* B C
87 Your] A; your B C
89 they're] A; they are B C
92 before-hand] A; beforehand B C
93 monstrous! Hang] A; monstrous —Hang B C
93 or Snipe] A; or a Snipe B C
95 mind] A; Mind B C
96 *Worthy*, your] A; *Worthy*! your B C
97 I'm] A; I am B C
98 Sir; you] A; Sir, you B C
100 Advices] A; Letters B C
101 ; the] A; : The B C
102 bear,] A; bear; but B C
104 you are] A; you're B C
105 Body? A; body. B; Body. C
107 cou'd] A C; coud B
108 Prejudice without] A C; prejudice, without B
109 shou'd] A B; shew'd C
111 me that] A; me, that B C
113 Nay, then Sir] A; Nay then, Sir B C
114 *Takes up a piece of the Letter.*] A; *Takes up a Bit.* B C
120 me!—Dear] A; me! Dear B C
121 pieces] A; Pieces B C
121 Letter, 'twill] A; Letter; 'twill B C
121 a hank upon] A; a Power over B C
122 hand, 'twas] A; Hand: 'Twas B C
127 Battel just] A; Battel, just B C
129 BALLANCE. 'Tis probable, I am satisfy'd] A; this speech is omitted in B C, Plume's speech continuing with the words, But I hope . . .
131 Account?] A; account. B; Account. C
132 no—Poor] A; no, poor B C
132 she is] A; she's B C
133 Company she] A; Company, she B C
136 pressing, the] A; pressing; the B C
138 Sir—] A; Sir!—
141 enough—] A; enough, B C
142 Women as] A; Women, as B C
142 Men forget] A; Men, forget B C
143 Acquaintance—But] A; Acquaintance?—But B C
143 come—where's] A; come, where's B
144 Fellow, I] A; Fellow? I B C
144 wou'd] A; would B C
147 *Horton's*, I'm] A; *Horton's*; I am B C
147 Hours] A; hours B C
148 shou'd] A; should B C
148 Company] A C; company B
150 Son; the] A; Son: The B C

ACT II. SCENE III

s.d. *one of the Mob*] A; *a Mob* B C
s.d. *hand, drunk*. KITE] A; *Hand drunk*—KITE B C
1 *refuse*] A; *refuse*, B C
4 *Hills and*] A; *Hills, and* B C
4 *Over the Hills, &c*] A; *Over, &c.* B C
5 *We all shall*] A; *We shall* B C
8 *Over the Hills, &c*] A; *Over, &c* B C
9 Boys—] A; boys! B C
9 live, drink] A; live; Drink B C
10 play; we] A; play: We B C
11 We're] A; We are B C
12 you're] A; you are B C
12 You're] A; You are B C
12 Emperour] A; Emperor B C
14 no Emperour] A; no Emperor B; Emperor C

18 I,] A; I; B C
18 pressing] A; Pressing B C
20 Done, you're] A; Done: You are B C
20 You're] A; you are B C
21 I'm] A; I am B C
22 No,] A; Ay, B C
26 *England*—That's] A; *England*, that's B C
27 'em all] A C; 'um all B
28 said! Faith: Huzza] A; said, faith; Huzza B C
28 *All Huzza*] A; *Huzza*! B C
29 heark'e] A; heark'ee B C
29 ever] A; never B C
31 *1st and 2d Mob.*] A; *Mob.* B C
31 No, no.] A; No, no, no. B C
32 that,] A; that; B C
33 the Mark (*He takes two Broad Pieces out of his Pocket*) See here, they're set in Gold (*gives one to each*)
1st Mob. (*Looking earnestly upon the Piece* The wonderful Works of Nature)] A; the Mark. See here, they are set in Gold. (*Takes two Broad Pieces out of his Pocket, gives one to each Mob*)
1st Mob. The wonderful Works of Nature! (*Looking at it*) B C
37 Here's B C] Her'es A
38 that Serjeant?] A; that, Serjeant? B C
39 O *Carolus*—] A; O! *Carolus*!—B C
39 *Ann*, that's]; *Ann*; That's B C
41 Scollard, Serjeant] A; Scollard—Serjeant B C
42 this?] A; This? B C
42 Compass of a Crawn] A; compass of a Crown B C
44 buying—'Tis] A; buying; 'tis B C
45 I present] A; I'll present B C them] A: 'em B
45 you both, you] A; you both: You B; ye both: You C
46 thing; put] A; thing. Put B C
46 them] A; 'em B C
47 I'm] A; I am B C
47 *over the Hills and far away.* (*Singing*)] A; over the Hills and far-away. B; over the Hills and far away. C
48 *sing and*] A; *sing, and* B C
49 *o'er*] B C; *o're* A
50 *Spain*;] A; *Spain*: B C
52 *Hill and*] A; *Hills, and* B C
54 ye; who] A: ye: Who B C
55 Hats; Ouns, off] A; Hats; Ounds off B
55 Hats; this] A; Hats: This B C
58 Lieutenant Captains] A; Lieutenant-Captains B C
58 too; Flesh, I'se] A; too: s'flesh! I'll B C
60 d'off] A; doff B C
60 *England*, my] A; *England*: My B C
64 Queen;] A; Queen: B C
64 them] A; 'em B C
64 now as] A; now, as B C
64 Volunteers under] A; Volunteers, under B C
66 have,] A; have: B C
67 Soldiers] A; Souldiers B C
69 Wauns] A; Wounds, B C
69 *Tummas*, What's] A; *Tummas*, what's B C
69 this? Are] A; this! are B C
70 Flesh, not] A; Flesh! not B
70 you, *Costar*?] A B; you *Costar* C
71 Wauns] A; Wounds B C
72 What,] A; What! B C
72 Ha,] A; ha, B C
72 Jest, Faith] A; Jest faith B C
73 Come, *Tummas*] A C; Come *Tummas* B
73 Whome] A; home B C
75 For] A; for B C
76 Captain—] A; Captain: B C
76 *Costar*—] A; *Costar*. B C
77 *going*] A; B C omit this stage direction

78 Nay, then] A; Nay then, B C
78 stay,] A; stay: B C
79 place for] A; place, for B C
80 you, and] A; you; and B C
80 *Chad's*, and] A; *Chad's*: And B C
81 relieved] A; reliev'd B C
83 Serjeant—] A; Serjeant? B C
83 you're] A; you are B C
85 sir, they] A; sir: They B C
86 them] A; 'em B C
87 Shot! *Tummas*.] A; Shot, *Tummas*! B C
88 what is] A; what's B C
90 Sir—But] A; Sir—but—B C
92 neither.] A; neither; B C
93 shot; but] A; shot: But B C
94 Pardon that] A; Pardon, that B C
97 Money?] B C; Money. A
98 brass] A; Brass B C
99 them] A C; 'em B
101 Wauns! If] A; Wounds, if B C
101 Pocket, but] A; Pocket but B C
104 look'e] A; look ye B C
105 too, nothing] A; too: Nothing B C
105 Picture that] A; Picture, that B C
108 Six-pence] A; Sixpence B C
110 you; those] A; you: Those B C
110 three and twenty] A; Three and Twenty B C
111 Six-pence] A; Sixpence B C
112 three and twenty] A; Three and Twenty B C
113 Six-pence] A; Sixpence B C
113 Latin] A; *Latine* B C
114 in the *Greek*] A B; In *Greek* C
115 Flesh, but] A; Flesh! but B C
115 *Tummas*, I] A; *Tummas*: I B C
116 Mayar] A; Mayor B C
116 ⟨*While they talk, the Captain and Serjeant whisper*⟩] A; *Captain and Serjeant whisper the while* B C
117 *Kite*; your] A; *Kite*—Your B C
117 Tricks] A C; Trick B
117 ruine] A; ruin B C
118 last, I] A; last—I B C
119 offers here to] A; offers to B C
120 you're] A; you are B C
121 Soldiers] A C; Souldiers B
122 Folks,] A; folks: B C
122 me or] A; me, or B C
125 Look'e you Rascal] A; Look'e, Rascal B C
125 Villain, if] A; Villain; if B C
127 Dog; come] A; Dog—Come B C
128 Nay, then we] A; Nay then, we B C
128 speak, your] A; speak; your B C
129 —And—] A;—and—B C
130 speak, you] A; speak; you B C
130 read; and] A; read—And B C
131 pieces] A; Pieces B C
134 Fellows like] A; Fellows, like B C
134 you;] A; you: B C
135 Villain, &c] A; Villain! B C
135 (*Beats the Serjeant off the Stage, and follows him out*)] A; (*Beats off the Serjeant, and follows*) B C
136 brave] A; Brave B C
136 Captain, huzza, a] A; Captain! Huzza! a B C
138 Now *Tummas*] A; Now, *Tummas* B C
138 beating] A; Beating B C
139 saw, Wauns, I] A; saw—Wounds, I B C
139 Month's] A; months B C
140 (*Re-enter* PLUME)] A; (*Enter* PLUME) B C
141 Dog! To] A; Dog, to B C
141 pretty] A; honest B C
141 you; Look'e] A; you—Look'e B C
142 Fellow, I] A; Fellow; I B C
143 Soldiers] A C; Souldiers B
143 Kidnapper, to] A; Kidnapper to B C
146 self,] A; self: B C
147 you or] A; you, or B C
147 go,] A; do; B C
148 Musket] A; Musquet B C
149 *Costar*, a] A; *Costar*: A B C
151 Pockets;] A; Pockets, B C
152 Oath that you] A; Oath you B C

152 listed, but] A; listed; but B C
153 Liberty] A; liberty B C
154 Captain, I Cod, I] A; Captain,—I Cod I B C
154 cannot] A; can't B C
155 Heart] A; heart B C
156 alway] A; always B C
156 Mind] A; mind B C
157 I'll tell you,] A; I'll you: B; I'll tell you: C
157 you're] A; You're B C
158 place] A; Place B C
159 ever, every] A; ever: Every B C
159 yours;] A; yours: B C
160 Purse full of] A; Purse of B C
162 Firelock, eh—] A; Firelock? eh!—B C
163 Wauns,] A; Wauns! B C
165 duna] A; do'na B C
166 Here, my Heroe] A; Here my Hero B C
166 earnest] A; Earnest B C
168 Duna] A; Do'na B C
168 (*Cries and*)] A; (*Crys, and*) B C
169 wull, I] A; wull—I B C
169 wull, Wauns] A; wull—Wauns B C
170 self;] A; self—B C
170 I'm] A; I am B C
172 hand—And] A; Hand, and B C
173 o're] A; o'er B C
173 command wherever] A; command it wherever B C
174 you if] A; you, if B C
175 part—] A; part? B C
176 cannot] A; canno B C
176 Captain, (*Crying*)] A; B C omit stage direction
177 e'ne] A; e'en B C
178 that] A; than B C
180 now] A; Now B C
186 well;] A; well: B C
186 Lads, now] A; Lads—Now B C
186 we will] A; we'll B C
186 sing *Over*] A; sing, *Over* B C
187 *Hills and*] A; *Hills*, *and* B C
189 *one to ten*] A; *One to Ten* B C
190 B C supply stage direction ⟨*Exeunt*

ACT III. SCENE I

s.d. PLUME *and* WORTHY] A; *Enter* PLUME and WORTHY B C
1 Can'nt] A; cannot B C
2 Fortunes, we] A; Fortunes: We B C
9 Letter you] A; Letter, you B C
10 Fortune-teller] A; Fortune-Teller B C
16 Year, and] A; Year; and B C
18 hundred; the] A; hundred—The B C
19 *Silvia*, with] A; *Sylvia* with B C
20 despise.] A; despise—B C
20 A SONG] A; this song is omitted in B C
43 What! Sneak] A; What sneak B C
43 o'] A; of B C
44 Complement! 'Sdeath,] A; Complement—'sdeath! B C
44 I'll] B C; I'd A
46 ha; ay] A; ha, ay B C
47 her.] A; her—B C
47 Military] A; military B C
49 Sir,] A; Sir! B C
50 Tit—] A; Tit. B C
51 show] A; shew B C
51 I'm] A; I am B C
51 Love] A; love B C
52 Here] A; here B C
54 *Rose with a Basket on her Arm, crying Chickens*] A; *and Chickens on her Arms in a Basket &c* B C
55 tender—young] A; tender, young B C
57 Chickens—] A; Chickens! B C
62 self;] A; self—B C
62 come] A; Come B C
63 my Child] A; B C omit my
64 Sarvice] A; service B C
66 see—Young] A; see; young B C

66 say?] A; say. B C
68 Bottom] A; bottom B C
70 hand,] A; Hand; B C
74 then; A; then, B C
75 Birds; pray] A; Birds—Pray B C
76 Sir, my] A; Sir: My B C
76 o' th'] A; o' the B C
77 Market, I] A; Market; I B C
79 hast ye,] A; haste, B C
79 liate a whome] A; lait hoame B C
79 *All this while* BULLOCK *whistles about the Stage*] A; *Whistles about the Stage* B C
80 *He tips the wink upon* KITE, *who returns it*] A; *Tips him the wink, he returns it* B C
81 *Rose*! You] A; *Rose*—You B C
81 Let] A; let B C
81 How] A; how B C
82 Sir—and] A; Sir, and B C
82 Crawn] A; Crown B C
83 Stracke o'] A; Strake of B C
84 Day] A; day B C
87 four-pence] A; Four-pence B C
89 on] A; of B C
89 Crawn] A; Crown B C
90 Bargain is] A; Bargain's B C
91 Dear] A; dear B C
92 con't] A; can't B C
93 indeed but] A; indeed, but B C
94 you shall bring home the Chickens,] A; Chicken, B C
97 pick] A; pick'd B C
99 things—But] A; Things; but B C
100 pray Sir] A; pray, Sir B C
101 Why 'tis] A; Why, 'tis B C
103 Digestion!] A; Digestion. B C
104 be?—] A; be? B C
106 Thickness] A; thickness B C
108 Fib] A; Fibb B C
108 believe—] A; believe. B C
108 —Eh, where's] A; Eh! Where's B C
109 *Ruose, Ruose Ruose*, 'sflesh] A; *Ruose*? *Ruose*! *Ruose*! 'sflesh B C
114 ruin'd; which] A; ruin'd—Which B C
115 she—] A; she?—B; she? C
116 Palisaders.] A; Palisadoes B C
120 way, I] A; way I B C
121 it; you] A; it—You B C
122 Gypsie] A; Gipsey B C
123 Year] A; Years B C
125 Pistols] A; Pistoles B C
125 Beauty made] A; Beauty, made B C
125 Page,] A; Page; B C
126 Pimping; I] A; Pimping. I B C
127 Brandy, and] A; Ratafia; and B C
128 Bailiff's] A; Bayliff's B C
128 Swearing—I] A; Swearing. I B C
133 Total will amount] A B; Total amount C
134 pray, what] A; pray what B C
135 Ambition—The] A; Ambition; the B C
138 I gad] A; egad B C
138 'twas] A; it was B C
138 I ever] A; ever I B C
139 To] A; to B C
140 *Savoy*—] A; *Savoy*. B C
140 Prison,] A; Prison; B C
141 Garrison,] A; Garrison; B C
143 again; but] A; again. But B C
147 Sister, do] A; Sister; do B C
148 Matter] A; matter B C
152 an't] A; an B C
154 o' th'] A; of the B C
155 Thou art] A; Tho'rt B C
155 a mad Fellow] A; mad, fellow B C
163 Luord] A; Lord B C
164 Gentleman, here] A; Gentleman here B C
166 did ye?] A; did you? B C
167 Lack-a-day] A; Lackaday B C
167 Only] A; only B C
169 Powder—Well, Friend] A; Powder. Well Friend B C
173 Battel, the] A; Battel—the B C
176 and I desire] A; and desire B C
178 Ay—And] A; Ay, and B C
178 ben't] A; been't B C
180 Friend—You] A; Friend, you B C

181 Compliment] A; Complement B C
185 Disdain.] A; Disdain; B C
186 better, I] A; better; I B C
186 much such] A; just such B C
187 Age; I]; A; Age I B C
188 me] A; my self B C
188 Disappointment, but] A; Disappointment; but B C
191 World; but] A; World. But B C
192 slowly, *Cupid*] A; slowly. *Cupid* B C
193 has] A; had B C
196 live yonder] A; live, yonder B C
198 Sash. I] A; Sash, I B C
201 sight;] A (in Harvard copy) B C; sight, A (in Yale, V & A, Bodley, Edinburgh and Leeds quartos) body] A; Body B C
215 Causes, Springs, or] A; Causes, or B C
223 Life! A; Life. B C
224 I'm] A; I am B C
225 Heark'e] A; Hark'e B C
227 body's] A; Body's B C
228 *vie*, I] A; *vie*! I B C
231 will—My] A; will. My B C
231 Dear] A; dear B C
231 forth, your] A; forth,—your B C
233 *Laconick*, a] A; *Laconick*! A B C
237 Ribbond] A; Ribbon B C
239 Pray Sir] A; Pray, Sir B C
245 reason] A; Reason B C
247 rid] A; must have rid B C
250 d'e] A; do you B C
250 Gentlemen, I] A; Gentlemen? I B C
250 kill'd;] A; kill'd, B C
251 Cannon-shot] A; Cannon Shot B C
251 six that I] A; six I B C
255 *Brazen*! A] A; *Brazen*, a B C
262 Tongue-Pad the] A; Tongue-Pad the B C
262 Chancery,] A; Chancery; B C
265 *Marjory*] A; *Margery* B C
265 Soul I] A; Soul, I B C
266 remember—But, Gentlemen (*Looking on his Watch*)] A; remember. (Looking on his Watch) But Gentlemen B C
267 presently, upon] A; presently upon B C
276 see—Sir] A; see; Sir B C
277 Business; but] A; Business—but B; Business—But C
278 *singing what she pleases*] A; *singing* B C
279 Lady;] A; Lady, B C
280 Side-saddle,] A; Side-saddle; B C
281 Tombs and] A; Tombs, and B C
281 Lions] A; Lyons B C
282 Sir—an't] A; Sir, an' B C
283 thro'] A; through B C
285 *showing*] A; *shewing* B C
288 by't] A; by it B C
291 Mangeree] A; Mangere B C
291 here; (*she takes*)] A; here. (*Takes*) B C
291 the] A; The B C
292 learnt] A; learn'd B C
293 Oho, the] A; Oho! The B C
293 Murder's] A; Murther's B C
294 Air?] A; Air. B C
295 Air, too] A; Air too B C
296 Snuff.] A; Snuff?
297 You'r] A; You are B C
297 Maid, and] A; Maid. And B C
305 O he's] A; Oh! he's B C
305 Gentleman as] A; Gentleman, as B C
306 ROSE. But I must beg your Worship's Pardon, I must go seek out my Brother Bullock ⟨*Runs off singing*⟩
308 BALLANCE. If all Officers took the same Method of Recruiting with this Gentleman, they might come in time to be Fathers as well as Captains of their Companies] A; B C omit
315 *on*] A; of B C
316 condemn'd] A; condemned B C

317 Oh,] A; O, B C
319 Child, are] A; Child! are B C
319 mad?—] A; mad—B C
319 *Ballance*, I] A; *Ballance* I B C
320 ha' n't] A B; han't C
322 you.] A; you.—B C
323 ROSE.] B C; ROSE, A
324 Sir; I] A; Sir—I B C
325 Sir.] A; Sir.—B C
326 wou'd but] A; wou'd—but B C
329 ROSE.] B C; ROSE, A

ACT III. SCENE II

2 Knots; or] A; Knots, or B C
6 Lace is] B C; Lace, is A
8 them] A; 'em B C
14 me as] A; me, as B C
14 Fault, the] A; Fault; the B C
15 mine tho'] A; mine, tho' B C
16 Week can] A; Week, can B C
17 Madam, his] A; Madam—His B C
18 Days—] A; Days. B C
19 Friend, the] A; Friend the B C
19 Captain, were] A; Captain were B C
19 ty'd on] A; ty'd upon B C
21 say, they] A; say—they B C
22 home] A; Home B C
32 Oh!] A B; O! C
35 fancy] A; Fansie B C
36 Assignation, I] A; Assignation I B C
38 True] A; Truth B C
38 Faith.] A; Faith! B C
38 I'll draw up all . . . *Princess of the* Severn *glide*] A; B C omit this part of Brazen's speech
45 I'm] A; I am B C
46 *Severn*, do] A; *Severn*—Do B C
47 melancholy] A C; Melancholy B
52 Campaigns] A; Campains B C
57 Madam, but] A; Madam—But B C
59 agreeable:] A; agreeable—B C
60 Madam, I] A; Madam,—I B C
60 Princess worth] A; Princess, worth B C
60 Fifty] A; fifty B C
61 me; the] A; me.—The B C
62 Love] A; love B C
63 Infidels, she] A; Infidels; she B C
64 me,] A; me; B C
65 time] A; Time B C
65 come, Hanging] A; come; Hanging B C
73 are you] A; Are your B; Are you C
76 *Worthy*,—your] A; *Worthy*, your B C
77 Fire!] A; Fire, B C
83 drunk?] A; drunk. B C
91 rigg'd] A C; rig'd B
92 the Frigot is called] A; she is call'd B C
93 Rate I] A; Rate, I B C
95 notice] A; Notice B C
98 but with an] A; but an B C
99 Wench or] A; Wench, or B C
100 heark'e my] A; heark'e, my B C
101 Love,—I] A; Love. I B C
101 tell'e] A; tell you B C
103 A Platoon!] A; Platoon, B C
107 Soh—] A; Soh! B C
107 I must] A; must I B C
107 sober and] A; sober, and B C
110 suppose.] A; suppose, Sir B C
112 Dear!] A; Dear.
113—Your] A; Your B C
113 Dear,] A; Dear? B C
114 mistaken, I] A B; mistaken I C
115 your's] A; yours B C
116 Sun's that] A; Sun's that B C
116 all, and] A C; all and B
121 Sir; For] A; Sir, for B C
123 Soh—Between] A; So, between B C
124 hands] A; Hands B C
124 yonder,—] A; yonder—B C
132 quiet, I] A; quiet—I B C
132 out.] A; out—B C
133 *do's*] A B; *does* C

134 *thee*,] A; *thee* B; Thee C
135 Madam, if] A; Madam.—B C
136 Poet; but] A; Poet.—But B C
136 show] A; shew B C
137 Madam, we'll] A; Madam,—we'll B C
137 us,] A; us; B C
138 (*Draws*, MELINDA shrieks)] A (*Draws* MELINDA ⟨Shrieking⟩) B C
139 *Worthy*, save] A; *Worth*! save B; *Worthy*! save C
139 Madmen] A; mad Men B C
139 *Runs off with* WORTHY] A; *Ex. with* WORTHY B C
140 ha,] A; ha! B C
140 Sir, and] A; Sir? and B C
141 Ravisher?] A; Ravisher. B C
142 you're] A; you are B C
145 Pray] A; pray B C
146 It cost my Enemies thousands of Lives, Sir] A; It cost me twenty Pistoles in *France*, and my Enemies thousands of Lives in *Flanders*. B C
147 Bargain] A B; bargain C
147 SILVIA *drest in*] A; SILVIA *in* B C
149 Dear, I'm] A; dear! I'm B C
151 presently—A; presently.—B C
152 *Wilfull*,] A; *Wilful*; B C
152 *Wilfull*] A; *Wilful* B C
153 *Wilfulls*] A; *Wilfuls* B C
154 *Wilfulls*] A; *Wilfuls* B C
155 present.] A C; present? B
156 the] A; this B C
157 shou'd;] A; stand, B C
158 Habitation beyond] A; Habitation, beyond B C
158 spot] A; Spot B C
162 but I intend] A C; but intend B
162 immediately—] A; immediately.—B C
163 shall have] A; has B C
164 you] A C; your B
166 A Corporal! A; Corporal! B C
169 me, you] A; me you B C
169 *Kisses her*] A; *Kisses* B C
171 Field-Officer] A; Field Officer B C
172 pho, I'll] A; pho! I'll B C
174 Sir? A; Sir. B C
176 done, I'll] A; done.—I'll B C
178 chuse,] A; chuse; B C
179 *Plume* that] A; *Plume*, that B C
183 day!] A; Day! B C
184 *Plume*, I'm] A; *Plume*! I'm B C
185 *Brazen*, I'm] A; *Brazen*! I'm B C
185 dare not] A B; dares not C
188 Captain—] A; Captain. B C
189 Serjeant here has] A; Serjeant has B C
190 Sot—] A; Sot.—B C
192 Banes—] A; Banes.—B C
194 first, I] A; first; I B C
195 free-born] A; Free-born B C
195 *Englishman* A] A; *English* Man B C
199 you, Captain] A B; you Captain C
202 Dog, give] A; Dog; give B C
202 Money Noble] A; Money, noble B C
204 Hold, hold, then] A; Then B C
205 won't] A; wont B C
206 presently; heark'e my Dear]. A; presently.—Heark'e, my dear. B C
208 I'm] A; I am B C
210 *Kite*?] A; *Kite*. B C
213 Pray Sir,] A; pray, Sir, B C
216 Image and Superscription of] A; Image of B C
216 Brother, two] A; Brother; two B C
217 Caliber] A; Caliver B C
217 like; sure] A; like: Sure B C
220 Variation] A; variation B C
220 Effa ut flat; my] C; fa ut flat; my A; Effa-ut Flatt: My B; Effa ut flatt: My C
221 so if] A; so, if B C
222 Noble] A; noble B C
223 Comrade if] A; Comrade, if B C
225 Ambition! There again,] A; Ambition there again! B C

226 Halberd] A; Halbert B C
227 already, pray noble] A; already: Pray, noble B C
229 What! Men] A; What, Men B C
229 another!] A; another. B C
230 do,] A; do; B C
231 fighting—But] A; fighting: But B C
233 Captain by] A C; Captain, by B
234 the t'other] A; the other B C
237 you're] A; you are B C
238 abroad, I] A; abroad; I B C
241 BRAZEN. (*Retiring*) Hold] A; BRAZEN. Hold B C
242 the Lady?] A; the Lady? (*Retiring*) B C
243 do, but] A; do—But B C
244 lye] A; Lye B C
244 *and is*] A; *who is* B C
244 *Mouth, takes*] A; *Mouth; takes* B C
244 *Arms, and*] A; *Arms and* B C
245 Hold—Where's] A; Hold, where's B C
248 Dear] A; dear B C
249 heart,] A; Heart, B; Heart. C
249 Dear] A; dear B C
249 (*Puts up*)] A; (*Putting up*) B C
250 *They embrace*] A; *Embrace* B C
251 You're] A; You are B C
253 afterwards—] A; afterwards.— B C
254 that] A; That B C
254 Lady that we] A; Lady we B C
254 o'] A; of B C
255 Morning, so] A; Morning—So B C
256 I'm] A; I am B C
257 nevertheless; her] A; nevertheless —Her B C
258 Pound you know will] A; Pound, you know, will B C
258 Convenience, I] A; Conveniency —I B C
260 Sport, curse ye] A; Sport. Curse you B C
260 Dear,—But] A; Dear, but B; dear, but C
260 again.] A; agen—B C
261 dear] A; Dear B C

ACT IV. SCENE I

1 Booby, you're] A; Booby? you are B C
2 Preferment] B C; Prefermeat A
4 you,] A; you; B C
5 Come throw] A; Come, throw B C
7 somebody] A; some body B C
8 of; this] A; of: This B C
10 Sweet-heart] A; Sweetheart B C
10 o'] A; of B C
11 Look'e, I'm] A; Look'e I'm B C
Relations; I] A; Relations:—I B C
12 he could play] A; he play'd B C
13 Tabor] A; Taber B C
13 for a Drum-Major] A; for Drum-Major B C
18 'um] A; 'em B C
21 here, *Rose*,] A; here? *Rose*! B C
21 Nurse's] A; Nurses B C
23 And] A; and B C
23 Well, honest] A; Well honest B C
24 Difference] A; difference B C
24 Horse Cart] A B; Horse and Cart C
26 Captain by] A; Captain, by B C
30 you; my] A; you, my B C
32 Yes, I] A; Yes I B C
32 the very Ribbands] A; the Ribbands B C
33 them] A; 'em B C
34 assure that] A; assure you, that B C
36 care] A; Care B C
38 matter I] A; matter, I B C
40 Soh!—and] Soh,!—and A; So!—And B C
43 Sir!] A; Sir,—B C
43 expect,—] A; expect—B C
43 but] A; But B C

45 You] A C; Yo B
45 care] A; Care B C
46 before-hand] A; beforehand B C
48 Wauns, *Ruose*] A; Wuns, *Rose* B; Wuns, *Ruose* C
50 sold him my] A; sold my B C
50 Chickens,—] A; Chickens.—B C
51 that, tho' there be an ugly Song of Chickens and Sparragus.] A; that. B C
53 What!] A; What, B C
53 *Wilfull*] A; *wilful* B C
56 little—] A; little. B C
58 Right] A; right B C
60–62 PLUME . . . Fellow—let her go, I say.
SILVIA. Do you let her go.] A; PLUME . . . Fellow.
SILVIA. Sir, I wou'd qualifie my self for the service.
PLUME. Hast thou really a Mind to the Service?
SILVIA. Yes, Sir; So let her go. B C (but C gives mind for Mind)
63–76 PLUME. *Entendez vous* . . . BULLOCK ⟨*Crying*⟩] A; in B C the following passage is substituted (C's variants are listed in square brackets)
ROSE. Pray, Gentlemen, don't be so violent.
PLUME. Come, leave it to the Girl's own Choice. [C omits.]—Will you belong to me or to that Gentleman?
ROSE. Let me consider, you're both very handsom [handsome C]
PLUME. Now the natural Unconstancy of her Sex begins to work.
ROSE. Pray, Sir, what will you give me?
BULLOCK. Don't be angry, Sir, that my Sister shou'd be Mercenary, for she's but young.
SILVIA. Give thee, Child!—Ill [I'll C] set thee above Scandal; you shall have a Coach with Six before and Six [six C] behind, an Equipage to make Vice fashionable, and put Vertue out of Countenance.
PLUME. Pho, that's easily done, I'll do more for thee, Child, I'll buy you a furbuloe Scarf, and give you a Ticket to see a Play.
BULLOCK. A Play, Wauns *Ruose* take the Ticket, and let's see the Show.
SILVIA. Look'e, Captain, if you won't resign, I'll go list with Captain *Brazen* this Minute.
PLUME. Will you list with me if I give up my Title?
SILVIA. I will.
PLUME. Take her: I'll change a Woman for a Man at any time.
ROSE. I have heard before, indeed, that you Captains us'd to sell your Men.
76 BULLOCK ([*Crying*]) Pray] A; BULLOCK. Pray B C (B C omit s.d.)
78 *West-Indies*] A; *West Indies* B C
79 *West-Indies*] A; *West Indies* B C
79 no, no] A; No, no B C
80 Hand, nor you,] A; Hand; nor you B C
80 do.—] A B; do—C
85 Captain's—] A; Captains; B; Captain's C
87 her,—She] A; her; she B C
88 what] A; What B C
89 Ah! Sir.] A; O! Sir, B; O! Sir! C
89 Drum-Major.] A; Drum-Major—B; Drum-Major.—C
91 but] A; But B C
91 ye] A; you B C
92 You're] A; you are B C
94 dear] A; Dear B C
95 Come, Brother] A; Come Brother B C
97 yes—and] A; Yes; and B C

98 Listing—money, if] A; listing Money; if B C
99 Wench I] A; Wench, I B C
99 mean; for] A; mean.— For B C
102 assur'd that I won't sell] A; assur'd I'd sell B C
103 Estate,—so] A; Estate.—So B C
104 list I] A; list, I B C
105 tell how you] A; tell you, how B C
106 point] A; Point B C
109 Security] A; security B C
115 Followers; the] A; Followers. The B C
115 Women, you know,] A; Women you know B C
116 where—gain] A; where; gain B C
117 you're] A; you are B C
117 Mistresses] A; Mistress B C
118 their] A; the B C
120 Men: So] A; Men—So B C
123 Fatigues] A; Fatigue B C
124 intollerable] A; intolerable B C
126 Debate—But] A; debate; but B C
130 place then] A; place, then B C
131 Company,] A; Company; B C
133 among] A; amongst B C
133 That] A; that B C
133 best.—] A; best. B C
139 Fault I] A; Fault, I B C
139 you, for] A; you; for B C
140 me I] A; me, I B C
141 me'twill] A; me, 'twill B C
142 will] A; can B C
145 Hand,—this] A; Hand, this B C
145 —and] A; —And B C
147 Friend—] A; Friend. B C
150 Noise] A; noise B C
150 Conduct if] A; Conduct, if B C
151 Circumstances] A; Circumstance B C
152 Head] A; head B C
152 impress'd] A; imprest B C
153 me—] A; me. B C
157 O fie,] A; O fye! B C
157 Soldier!—wou'd] A; Soldier! Wou'd B C
158 lye] A B; lie C
159 No, Faith, I am] A; No faith, I'm B C
159 imagines,] A; imagines; B C
161 Religion; the] A; Religion—The B C
162 mine which] A; mine, which B C
162 undesign'd to] A; undesign'd, to B C
163 hypocritical;] A; hypocritical. B C
165 lye] A B; lie C
170 Confident, we] A; Confident: We B C
171 Assistance] A C; assistance B
172 Cholick; A; Collick—B C
172 I'm] A; I am B C
173 help] A; Help B C
174 Madam,] A; Madam! B C
175 only—] A; only, B C
176 Town, I] A; Town I B C
176 Ease] A; ease B C
178 Madam,] A; Madam; B C
179 Cause] A; cause B C
183 Cause or] A; Cause, or B C
185 Husbands, our] A; Husbands our B C
186 'um] A; 'em B C
187 degree] A; Degree B C
188 Servant, you] A; Servant: You B C
188 five hundred Pound] A; 500 *l.* B C
189 Foot] A; foot B C
191 extremely] A; extreamly B C
191 Design that I] A; Design I B C
194 Advantage] A; advantage B C
194 you, 'twill] A; you: 'Twill B C
194 Humour] A; humour B C
196 five hundred] A; Five Hundred B; Five hundred C
196 Pound the Day] A; Pound upon my Day B C
199 Confident] A; Confidant B C
201 O, *Lucy*,] A; O *Lucy*! B
201 longer—] A; longer: B C
202 know that] A; know, that B C
203 Curiosity which] A Curiosity, which B C

203 dear; that] A; dear: That B C
204 Bosom-favourites] A; Bosom Favourites B C
205 surprising] A B; surprizing C
206 surprising] A; surprizing B C
207 surprising] A; surprizing B C
209 surprizing, he] A; surprizing: he B C
210 Maid.] A; Maid! B C
211 Maid—Come] A; Maid! come B C
211 nothing! Dear] A; nothing!—Dear B C
213 Thought] A; thought B C
215 Why, I] A; Why I B C
218 Power] A; power B C
220 *Lucy*, but] A; *Lucy*; but B C
221 Life; he] A; Life—He B C
224 to day—He] A; to day, he B C
225 incourag'd] A; encourag'd B C
228 off. 'Sdeath, I] A; off: 'sdeath! I B C
230 slave him.] A; use him! B C
232 you, Men] A; you; Men B C
232 scarce; and] A; scarce, and B C
236 hot,—You] A; hot—You B C
237 Walks where] A; Walks, where B C
237 late] A; lately B C
239 me, that] A; me that B C
241 Madam;] A; Madam: B C
241 here, because] A B; here because C
242 Place] A; place B C
246 is as free for me as you, Madam, and broad enough for us both.] A; is broad enough for us both. B C
248 *hand*,] A; *Hand*; B C
248 *enter Brazen, who takes*] A; *Brazen takes* B C
249 *Melinda about The Middle*] A; *her round the Waste* B C
250 What!] A; What, B C
250 Here] A; here B C
250 me! My Dear.] A; me, my dear! B C
251 Insolence?] A; Insolence! B C
252 LUCY ⟨*Runs* to BRAZEN⟩ Are . . . *Worthy*?] A; LUCY Are . . . *Worthy*? ⟨To BRAZEN⟩ B C
254 Adso,] A; Odso! B C
255 turn'd, my] A; turn'd—My B C
256 pardon] A; Pardon B C
256 you're] A; you are B C
266 shot] A; Shot B C
266 ha'] A; have B C
266 mine—Courage] A; mine: Courage B C
267 Dear] A B; dear C
267 War—But] A; War; but B C
269 Sir,] A; Sir! B C
270 show] A; shew B C
272 me; 'sdeath, why] A; me: 'sdeath! why B C
273 that is] A; that's B C
274 Royal; don't] A; Royal: Don't B C
274 Man,] A; Man; B C
275 own, I tell'e] A; own I tell you B C
276 Passion,] A; Passion: B C
276 the] A; The B C
276 sign] A; Sign B C
277 Madness; that] A; Madness. That B C
277 Rogue, *Kite*, began] A; Rogue *Kite* began B C
279 Part] A; part B C
282 her.] A; her? B C
283 Logician if] A; Logician, if B C
284 Fools, there's] A; Fools: There's B C
286 Conduct; Whim] A; Conduct—Whim B C
286 Whim, hurries them] A; Whim hurrys 'em B; whim hurry's em C
286 them] A; 'em B C
286 on, like] A; on like B C
288 sport, *Kite*] A; Sport—*Kite* B C
288 Hour] A; hour B C

ACT IV. SCENE II

s. d. *Chamber*.] A; *Chamber*; B C

s.d. *Habit, and*] A; *Habit sitting* B C
s.d. *the Table*] A; *a Table* B C
1 gain'd] A B; gaiu'd C
3 Tide–waiter] A; Tyde–waiter B C
5 Granadeers—And] A; Granadeers; and B C
5 Sistem] A; System B C
7 Shoemaker] A; Shoomaker B C
7 already,] A; already; B C
8 Dragoons, I] A; Dragoons—I B C
9 Lady Mr.] A; Lady, Mr. B C
11 Ay, but] B C; Ay, But A
13 stroak] A; Stroke B C
15 fear you] A; fear that you B C
16 break *Melinda*'s Windows] A; break Windows B C
17 Post—] A; Posts. B C
18 *Ticho*, mind] A; Mind B C
19 cunning] A; Cunning B C
20 learn'd] A; Learned B C
21 Master *Coppernose*,] A; Master, B C
23 Perhaps, that] A; Perhaps that B C
24 Look'e] A; Look ye B C
24 Let] A; let B C
27 forty fold. You're] A; forty fold —Your B; forth-fold—Your C
27 Countryman—You are] A; Countryman, you're B C
32 *Forceps*! What's] A; *Forceps*, what's B C
33 Signs; there's] A; Signs: There's B C
36 Cannons Bullets] A; Cannon Bullets? B C
39 Sir, your] A; Sir—Your B C
43 Arrears?] A C; arrears! B
44 five hundred] A; Five Hundred B C
47 hand] A; Hand B C
48 pardon] A; Pardon B C
49 fifty] A; Fifty B C
49 Fortnight's] A; Fortnights B C
51 So am I, Sir, among] A; Sir, I am above 'em, among B C
53 grand] A; Grand B C
53 ten] A; Ten B C
53 Day] A; day B C
54 Servants; 'tis] A; Servants—'Tis B C
54 fix'd] A; Fixt B C
56 be gone] A C; begone B
57 What, what] A; What! what B C
59 Hour] A; hour B C
61 Pen'worth] A; Pennyworth B C
63 you—What's a] A (Science Museum Quarto; copy text reads: What 'sa); you what's a B C
64 Fortune; follow] A; Fortune—Follow B C
64 him: And] A; him;—And B C
65 Children—An] A; Children; an B C
66 time—] A; time B C
67 Gentleman you say! With] A; Gentleman, you say, with B C
67 Cane, pray] A; Cane! Pray B C
69 Head, with] A; Head with B C
70 But pray, of] A; And pray of B C
71 see—He's] A; see, he's B C
71 Excise, a] A; Excise, or a B C
73 But] A; but B C
73 Your] A; your B C
76 Right, he'll call] A; He'll call B C
78 O, there] A; O there B C
78 *Tom a Lincoln*] A; *Tom o'Lincoln* B C
79 *Telltroth*] A; Tell-troth B C
79 *Tom o'Bedlam*, *Tom*] A; *Tom a Bedlam*, and *Tom* B C
79 *Fool*— ⟨*Knocking at the Door.*⟩ Be gone—An Hour hence precisely —] A; *Fool*—Be gone—An hour hence precisely ⟨*Knocking at the Door*⟩ B C
81 say he'll] A; say, he'll B C
82 certainly, and] A; certainly—And B C
82 Answer—You] A; answer you B C
82 know, and] A; know—And B C
83 Dial,] A; Dial; B C

86 *Behind*〉 Well done] A; B C place s.d. at end of sentence.
88 What! My] A; What my B C
88 *Pluck*, the] A; *Pluck* the
88 Butcher—] A; Butcher,—B C
91 Master Conjurer—Here's] A; Mr. Conjurer, here's B C
93 beforehand.] A; beforehand.—B C
94 then;] A; then, B C
97 Man-in-the-Moon) A; Man in the Moon B C
98 you the) A; you, the B C
99 Sun, don't) A; Sun: Don't B C
100 Moon, I) A; Moon I B C
102 hand—You are] A; Hand—You're B C
104 True—I] A; True, I B C
106 Ox, may] A; Ox may B C
106 Man; and] A; Man, and B C
110 Patience] A; patience B C
110 General,] A; General; B C
113 Patience] A; patience B C
114 absence] A; Absence B C
115 Worship,] A; Worship! B C
116 Nay, then I] A; Nay then, I B C
117 Doctor.] A; Doctor—B; Doctor.—C
118 Sir,] A; Sir! B C
118 do] A; Do B C
119 hurry'd—] A; hurry'd? B C
120 rate—] A; rate? B C
121 the] A; their B C
125 Half Crown] A; Half-Crown B C
127 then, once more] A; then once more B C
128 hand] A; Hand B C
134 Man call'd] A; Man, call'd B C
137 errant] A; arrant B C
137 Halbard—the] A; Halbard—The B; Halbard The C
140 a hundred] A; an Hundred B C
141 Minute] A; minute B C
141 Mercer, not] A; Mercer not B C
142 Oons,] A; Oons! B C
142 has;] A; has, B C
143 it? And] A; it, and B C
145 Discharge—] A; Discharge. B C
146 'Flesh] A; 'sflesh B C
147 half] A; Half B C
149 Danger] A; danger B C
151 you're] A; your B C
153 Passion] A; Passion. B C
154 they're] A; they are B C
154 again] A; agen B C
154 See—Did] A; see, did B C
160 second] A; Second B C
161 third] A; Third B C
161 third] A; Third B C
162 Shot; you] A; Shot, you B C
163 Cleaver] A; Clever B C
165 the general] A; general B C
167 Limb—] A; Limb, B C
167 do't—I'll do't] A; do't, I'll do't B C
170 What] A; what's B C
170 Thoughts? The] A; Thoughts, the B C
172 can't] A C; can B
174 ha' done—] A; have done; B C
175 Only] A; only B C
175 this—You'll] A; this, you'll B C
175 a half] A; half B C
175 hence—That's all—Farewel] A; hence, that's all, farewel B C
177 Pray what] A; What B C
178 pray.] A; pray? B C
179 Pound] A; Pounds B C
179 Year, beside] A; Year! besides B C
180 Pound] A; Pounds B C
180 and half] A; an a half B C
182 so troublesome—Here's] A; troublesome, here's B C
184 I tell you in] A; I tell in] B; I'll tell you C
186 hand] A; Hand B C
187 Pocket—He'll] A; Pocket; he'll B C
188 Loyn] A; Line B; Loin C
190 us—] A; us! B C
191 true, things] A; true—things B C
194 Sister, Women] A; Sister—Women B C

194 Preferment; make] A; Preferment —make B C
195 Gentleman—His] A; Gentleman, his B C
196 P] A; P. B C
197 to, she] A; to—she B C
198 haleing] A; halling B C
200 drives—] A; drives. B C
201 Pocket?] A; Pocket. B C
205 ⟨*Behind with . . .*⟩] A; B C place stage direction at end of sentence.
207 Silks,] A; Silks. B C
213 Madam, ⟨To Lucy⟩] A; B C place s.d. at end of sentence.
215 or with the] A; or the B C
217 both;] A; both, B C
218 Stars, when] A; Stars; when B C
219 hand] A; Hands B C
220 account] A; Account B C
222 Oh!] A; Oh B C
222 us—dear] A; us! Dear B C
222 let us] A; let's B C
224 Fool. Do] A; Fool; do B C
224 I'm] A; I am B C
226 Senses?—Come, show] A; Senses? Come, shew B C
231 Ha, ha, ha,] A; Ha, ha! B C
231 pray] A; Pray B C
233 Look'e,] A B; Look'e C
233 Lady,—the] A; Lady—The B C
234 body] A; Body B C
235 cannot] A; can't B C
236 do] A; Do B C
239 'em] A; them B C
240 show] A; shew B C
240 Tryal] A; Trial B C
240 Here, you] A; Here you B C
240 *Cacodemon*] A; *Cacodemo* B C
241 *fuego*, exert] A; *Plumo*—Exert B C
241 Power,—draw] A; Power, draw B C
242 the proper] A; Proper B C
242 Character] A; Characters B C
243 hand writing] A; Hand writing B C
243 Do] A; do B C
243 Motions,—] A; Motions—B C
243 one, two, three—] A; one,—two three B C
245 fetch] A C; fetcht B
246 fetch] A C; fetcht B
247 Hand-writing] A; Hand Writing B C
250 Sirrah—] A; Sirrah. B C
250 Oh! oh! the Devil . . . I'm sure the Blood comes—] A; B C omit
262 but there's your] A; There's your B C
263 Paper—behold—] A; Paper, behold—B C
264 wonderful—My] A; wonderful! my B C
267 now that will] A; now will B C
267 out-lie] A; out-lye B C
267 Devil.] A; Devil! B C
268 us, People] A; us; People B C
269 Faces—] A; Faces.—B C
271 Paper— ⟨*Takes out Paper and folds it*⟩ then] A; B C place stage direction at end of speech.
273 Madam,—] A; Madam—B C
274 *writes, and Lucy*] A; *writes*, LUCY B C
275 same, the] A; same—the B C
278 Madam, the] A; Madam—The B C
279 Demon] A; *Daemon* B C
279 Lies] A; Lyes B C
280 I'm] A; I am B C
280 pray what account] A; pray, what Account B C
283 fixt] A; fix'd B C
284 so] A; So B C
285 Morning you] A; Morning, you B C
286 Gentleman who] A; Gentleman, who B C
287 Travel. His] A; Travel, his B C
290 the t'other—] A; the other.—B C
290 in] A; In B C
290 travels he] A; travels, he B C
291 abroad;] A; abroad, B C
293 he is] A; he's B C

293 is, a] A; is a B C
296 Madam,—] A; Madam—B C
296 so: A] A; so—A B C
298 Ten, about] A; Ten—about, B C
299 Tea drinking] A; Tea-drinking B C
301 Here, Doctor] A; Here Doctor B C
303 O!) A; Oh, B C
303 Madam,] A; Madam! B C
305 besides, I] A; besides I B C
307 Pray,] A; O pray, B C
307 first.] A; first! B C
308 *Enter* PLUME *and* WORTHY *laughing*] A; *Enter* WORTHY *and* PLUME B C
309 KITE. Ay, you may well . . . PLUME. No more . . . a Wit] A; B C omit these four speeches.
318 that you ever] A; that ever I B C
319 Traveller you] A; Traveller, you B C
326 off—I] A; off, I B C
328 Gunpowder—thus] A; Gunpowder, thus B C
329 fortify] A; fortifie B C
330 and] A; And B C
330 Lines.] A; Lines! B C
331 You] A; you B C
336 Name, where] A; Name—where B C
338 —'Tis] A; 'tis B C
339 some pitiful place] A; some place B C
339 of *Scotland*] A; in *Scotland* B C
340 Right! I] A; Right—I B C
341 marry'd.—] A; marry'd—B C
341 I've] A; I have B C
343 Chollick] A; Collick B C
345 o' th'] A; of the B C
347 Love Letters] A B; Love—Letters C
348 o' th'] A; of the B C
351 Contents, that] A; Contents! that B C
358 *in 's*] A; *in his* B C
360 Place] A; place B C
360 —Here—] A; —here.—B C
361 and] A; And B C
364 Doctor,] A; Doctor! B C
365 it—and] A; it, and B C
365 I'm] B C; 'Im A
366 Pho,] A; Pho! B C
366 it,] A; it! B C
366 if] A; If B C
366 Jilt—] A; Jilt! B C
367 Damn] A; damn B C
369 How!—then] A; How! then B C
369 I will] A; I'll B C
370 *Lucy*'s] A B; *Lucy*'s. C
372 Certainly, 'tis] A; Certainly—'tis B C
376 see,] A; see; B C
379 plain, they're] A; plain they're B C
380 Letter which] A; Letter, which B C
381 Country?] A; Country. B C
382 show'd] A; shew'd B C
383 now, I once intended it for another use, but I think I have turn'd it now to better advantage] A; now. B C
387 angelick] A; Angelick B C
387 —poor *Silvia*] A; : Poor *Silvia*! B C
388 Captain—ha,] A; Captain, ha B C
389 ha; come] A; ha,—Come B C
391 Hopes] A; hopes B C
395 *sallies*] A; Sallys B C
400 *Alarms*,] A; Alarms; B C
402 A omits, B C supply stage direction *exeunt*

ACT V. SCENE I

s.d. ACT. V. SCENE, *an Antichamber, with a Perrywig, Hat and Sword upon the Table*] A; this scene is omitted in B C

ACT V. SCENE II

1 born] A; born, B C
3 Army;] A; Army, B C

4 Abroad] A; abroad B C
5 Grains] A C; Grain B
5 Home] A; home B C
7 you; shall] A; you—Shall B C
10 Officers we] A; Officers, we B C
11 Wife] A; Wives B C
12 Daughter.—] A; Daughters— B C
15 Life that] A; Life, that B C
15 Whore—this] A; Whore. This B C
18 body] A; Body B C
18 O! here] A; Oh here B C
19 come.] A; come! B C
19 *Prisoners, Constable*] A; *Prisoners; Constable* B C
21 Sir; the] A; Sir—The B C
22 Gentleman, for] A; Gentleman: for B C
24 wait] A; Wait B C
25 Ex. *Const.* &c] A; Ex. *Constable and Watch* B C
26 occasion] A; Occasion B C
27 Satisfaction] A B; satisfaction C
29 Behaviour.—] A; Behaviour—B C
31 you not] A; not you B C
32 Goose-Cap] A; Goosecap B C
35 you're] A; you are B C
36 Sorrow] A; sorrow B C
39 Bed side] A; Bed-side B C
41 Ministers] A; Minister B C
43 prating] A; Prating B C
43 Fool; your] A; Fool—Your B C
44 Understanding, pray what] A; Understanding; pray what B C
46 that, you know, is] A; that you know is B C
50 Sacred, our] A; sacred—Our B
50 Sword,] A; Sword B C
50 , you know,] A; you know B C
51 down, the] A; down—The B C
52 leap] A; Leap B C
52 Whore, the] A; Whore—The B C
53 Bed] A; bed B C
58 show] A; shew B C
59 it] A; it. B C
61 Coffee-men] A; Coffeemen B C
62 Groom Porters] A; Groom-Porters B C
62 *London*, for] A; *London*; for B C
62 red] A; Red B C
63 Sword *bien troussee*] A; Sword, a Hat *bien troussee* B C
64 Button; Picket] A; Button; Piquet B C
67 Captain] A; Capt. B C
67 *Pinch*;] A; *Pinch*: B C
68 Pinch; in] A; Pinch. In B C
74 Sir; here] A; Sir—Here B C
76 Worship, don't] Worship don't B C
77 Hurt,] A; hurt; B C
80 Gentlemen, rob] A; Gentlemen! rob B C
80 Freedom and] A; Freedom, and B C
81 'tis] A; 'Tis B C
82 Heark'e] A C; Heark'ye B
82 Constable—(*Whispers the Constable*)] A; Constable. 〈*Whispers him*. B C
83 Sir,—] A; Sir—B C

ACT V. SCENE III

s.d. SCENE *changes to* MELINDA'S *Apartment*] A; SCENE, MELINDA'S *Apartment* B C
s.p. *MELINDA*] A; *Enter* MELINDA B C
1 ten exactly;] A; Ten exactly. B C
2 and] A; And B C
6 Occasion] A; occasion B C
10 for it;] A; for't, B C
14 Country than] A; Country, than B C
17 barbarous Nations] A; barbarous of Nations B C
19 while—I] A; while; I B C
22 Debt] A; debt B C
25 O] A; Oh B C
25 *Worthy*,] A; *Worthy*! B C
26 Servitude; how] A; Servitude: How B C

27 Advantage] A; advantage B C
27 Innocence, and] A; Innocence and B C
31 Visits, remember] A; Visits; Remember B C
34 Madam—that] A; Madam, that B C
35 nothing, tis] A; nothing—'Tis B C
36 forget; you] A; forget: You B C
37 you—Put] A; you; put B C
37 balance] A; ballance B C
39 adventering] A; adventuring B C
39 handsomly] A; handsomely B C
40 *Lent*] A; Lent B C
40 over—Here's] A; over, here's B C
43 Poyson] A; Poison B C
43 *Enter Servant*] A; *Enter a Servant* B C
45 I'm] A; I am B C
45 Country-house] A; Country House B C
46 *Silvia*, I] A; *Silvia*; I B C
46 easie till] A; easy, till B C
49 full, but] A; full; but B C
49 Gallant] A; gallant B C
51 overtaken; and] A; overtaken, and B C
53 *Exit* WORTHY *leading*] A; *exit leading* B C

ACT V. SCENE IV

s.d. PLUME *and*] A; *Enter* PLUME *and* B C
2 at] A; in B C
4 hands] A; Hands B C
8 never] A; ne'er B C
9 Gypsies] A; Gipsies B C
10 Turkey; here's] A; Turkey—Here's B C
11 *Brazen*—Sir] A; *Brazen*, Sir B C
11 BRAZEN, *reading*] A; BRAZEN *reading* B C
14 Dear; what] A; dear: What B C
hand] A; Hand B C
16 thousand] A; Thousand B C
18 Dear] A; dear B C
18 twenty thousand] A; Twenty Thousand B C
20 Dear] A; dear B C
20 me,] A; me; B C
21 Play-house] A; Playhouse B C
22 A] A; a B C
22 Play-house] A; Playhouse B C
24 Dear—For] A; dear—for B C
31 But, you know, a] A; But you know a B C
32 Play-house] A; Playhouse B C
35 Play-house] A; Playhouse B C
35 So by] A; So, by B C
36 the] A; a B C
37 twenty thousand] A; Twenty Thousand B C
39 twenty thousand] A; Twenty Thousand B C
43 Presently, we're] A; Presently, We're B C
44 For fear . . . me for ever yours] A; For fear . . . me ever yours B C, which print the letter in italics
48 And] A; and B C
48 hand] A; Hand B C
49 Dear; her] A; Dear—Her B C
49 now you] A; now, you B C
53 way that] A; way, that B C
56 Secrets—] A; Secrets. B C
57 boot, and] A; boot and B C
59 shall,] A; shall: B C
59 she is] A; she's B C
60 *Silvia*; we] A; Silvia, we B C
65 hand] A; Hand B C
67 the *Elisian*] A; *Elysian* B; the *Elysian* C
69 now, she] A; now; she B C
73 hand] A; Hand B C
74 Minute] A; minute B C
75 Country House] A; Country-house B C
76 Minute] A; minute B C
76 s. d. *a Servant*] A; *Servant* B C
77 Sir, ⟨To *Worthy*.⟩ Madam] A; Madam B C

77 word that] A; word, that B C
78 her;] A; her, B C
81 off?] A; off! B C
82 put-off] A; Put-off B C
85 now, I] A; now I B C
85 Water side] A; Water-side B C
86 Up, or] A; Up or B C
91 Hall, the] A; Hall; the B C

ACT V. SCENE V

s.d. *Justice*,] A; *Justice*: B C
s.d. SCALE, SCRUPLE, *upon*] A; SCALE, and SCRUPLE upon B C
s.d. *Bench*. Constable] A; *Bench*: Constable B C
s.d. *advance to the Front of the Stage*.] A; *advance forward* B C
1 Pray, who] A; Pray who B C
4 *Scruple*,] A; *Scruple*; B C
6 Sir, I'm] A; Sir! I am B C
8 same, for] A; same; for BC
9 we're] A; we are B C
9 Staff-Officers] A; Staff Officers B C
12 exercise—Suppose] A B; exercise Suppose C
13 Musquet] A; Musket B C
13 now,] A; now. B C
13 *on his*] A; *on's* B C
14 I'm] A; I am B C
16 Musquet] A; Musket B C
16 t'other] A; the other B C
17 Adso,] A; Adso! B C
18 o'] A; of B C
20 will,—] A; will—B C
29 thank'e] A; thank you B C
30 me,] A; me. B C
34 an't] A; an B C
34 ye] A; you B C
35 What] A; what B C
36 an't] A; an B C
39 an't] A; an B C
40 truly!] A; truly— B C
45 speak;] A; speak, B C
45 nothing—] A; nothing. B C
46 him,] A; him; B C
47 besides his] A; besides, he's B C
48 high,] A; high; B C
48 Box, Wrestle] A; box, wrestle B C
49 County,] A; County; B; Country; C
50 Sabbath-Day] A; Sabbath-day B; Sabbath Day C
51 lie] A; lye B C
51 lie an't] A; lye, an B C
52 natur'd pains-taking] A; natur'dst pains-taking'st B C
54 Wife and] A; Wife! and B C
54 you] A; You B C
58 Hark'e] A; Heark'e B C
59 and Children] A; and five Children B C
61 Partridges] A; Partridge B C
62 Miles] A; Mile B C
63 Nay] A; nay B C
63 Gunning he] A; Gunning, he B C
66 *Ballance*.] A; *Ballance*! B C
67 Reason] A; reason B C
67 away—You] A; away; you B C
68 you're] A; you are B C
69 should] A; shou'd B C
72 next; that] A; next; That B C
72 feeding] A; Feeding B C
73 Beggars] A B; beggars C
75 loose] A; lose B C
75 Teeming Time if] A; teaming time, if B; teeming time, if C
79 *the Man*] A; *him* B C
81 Gun-powder] A; Gunpowder B C
87 Colepits] A; Cole-pits B C
91 Worships, this] A; Worships this B C
92 a Livelihood] A; Livelihood B C
92 under-ground] A; under ground B C
93 said *Kite*—] A; said, *Kite*, B C
93 Besides, the] A; besides the B C
94 Right!] A; Right, B C
95 neighbouring] A; Neighbouring B C
96 *Stafford* five] A; *Stafford*, five B C

96 under-ground] A; under Ground B C
100 Marry'd] A; marry'd B C
105 Worship, she's] A; Worship shes B C
98 We] A; we B C
110 Soldier] A C; Souldier B
111 Couple—Pray] A; Couple! pray B C
111 Captain, will] A; Captain will B C
113 *Kite*—Will] A; *Kite*, will B C
115 Sea side] A; Sea-side B C
116 self, we'll] A; self we'll B C
116 Body] A; body B C
118 Man] A; Man. B C
119 Now Captain] A; Now, Captain B C
120 ⟨*Enter*⟩] B C; A omits leading bracket
120 Const.] A; *Constable* B C
121 O] A; Oh! B C
121 *Pinch*—I'm] A; *Pinch*, I am B C
122 Well Sir] A; Well, Sir B C
124 Farthing] A; farthing B C
129 Whoremaster] A; Whore-master B C
133 hazard] A; hazzard B C
134 day] A; Day B C
140 (*Plume reads Articles of War against Mutiny and Desertion.*)] A; [PLUME *reads the Articles of War* B C
143 me, and] A; me; and B C
145 Look'ee] A; Look'e B C
145 Spark] A C; Sark B
145 Word] A; word B C
145 more and] A; more, and B C
147 tiresom] A; tiresome B C
148 *Huffcap*—But] A; *Huffcap*, but B C
155 mad,—] A; mad—B C
157 more,—] A; more—B C
159 No Faith] A; No, Faith B C
160 first,] A B; first ‘ C
161 consider, my] A; consider my B C
162 Country; I'm] A; Country, I'm B C
163 loss] A; Loss B C
164 it] A C; he B
164 does. Captain] A; does; Captain B C
165 Minute, I'll] A; Minute I'll B C
167 whilst] A; while B C
168 Sir,—] A C; Sir—B
168 Silence Gentlemen] A; Silence, Gentlemen B C
169 now, Captain] A; now Captain B C
170 account] A B; Account C
170 whatsoever.—Bring] A; whatsoever. Bring B C
172 more, an't] A; more an't B C
173 two] A C; too B
176 allows] A; allow'd B C
176 Gains] A B; gains C
178 get] A; go B C
179 Guineas, but] A B; Guineas but C
179 me.—This] A; me, this B; me; this C
184 Man,—and] A; man, but B; Man, but C
184 and now that] A; but now since that B C
187 don't] A C; dont B
188 Ransom] A; Ransome B C
190 agreed.] A; agreed! B C
192 ay; Sir,—] A; ay—Sir. B C
193 you, or] A; you? Or B C
194 Staff as] A; Staff, as B C
194 *The Constable*] A; *Constable* B C
196 Court;—] A; Court—B C
196 Captain you] A; Captain, you B C
198 believe, without] A; believe without B C
198 *Omnes*] A; *omnes* B C

ACT V. SCENE VI

s.d. SCENE *changes to the Fields*, BRAZEN *leading in* LUCY *mask'd*] A; SCENE, *the Fields*.

Enter BRAZEN leading in LUCY mask'd B C
1 *Arm, parts* BRAZ. and LUCY.] A; *Arm* B C
2 Choice] A; choice B C
2 *offering the Pistols*] A; *going between 'em and offering them* B C
3 charg'd, my dear?] A; charg'd, my dear. B; charg'd my dear. C
6 way, and] A; way—and B C
9 Pistols;— A; Pistols—B C
9 pray] A; Pray B C
10 me and] A; me, and B C
10 dam't] A; dam it B C
14 then Fire] A C; then, Fire B
15 Cannon; Sir, don't] A; Cannon, Sir; don't B C
16 upon't; let] A; upon't. Let B C
16 see,] A; see. B C
16 *Takes a Pistol*] A; *Takes one* B C
16 and] A; And B C
17 paces] A; Paces B C
18 shot] A; Shot B C
19 I be] A; I am B C
24 LUCIA.]; *Lucia,* A.
26 take] A; Take B C
26 Huzza,] A; Huzza! B C
27 d'ye] A; D'ye B C
29 now?—] A; now! B C
30 LUCIA.]; *Lucia,* A; *Luc.* B C
32 safe;] A; safe. B C
32 you,—but] A; you; but B C
34 would] A; wou'd B C
37 LUCIA.]; *Lucia,* A.
41 LUCIA.]; *Lucia,* A.
41 Towns end] A B; Town's end C
42 body] A; Body B C
44 Fathers!] A; Father's! B C
44 this] A; This B C
46 *talking with his Steward*] A; *and Steward* B C
50 *London*, was] A; *London* was B C
51 white, trimm'd] A; white trim'd B C
53 body] A; Body B C
55 dont, go] A; dont; go B C
55 Dining Room] A; Dining-Room B C
57 shall.] A; shall.—B C
58 man] A; Man B C
60 Consent.—] A; Consent. B C
61 Deed; and] A; Deed—And B C
61 this, I] A; this I B C
64 imposed] A; impos'd B C
67 presently.] A; presently—B C
69 Souldier] A; Soldier B C
70 suppose, with] A B; suppose with C
72 Common] A B; common C
73 Souldiers ?] A; Soldiers B C
75 presume.] A; presume? B C
76 Faith,—] A; Faith, B C
76 Bed,] A; Bed—B C
77 layn] A; lain B C
82 safe, I] A; safe I B C
82 Now Captain] A; Now, Captain B C
83 grounded;] A; grounded, B C
84 said that I] A; said I B C
84 and I] A; and so I B C
86 for] A; For B C
86 reason?] A; Reason? B C
89 pound] A; Pound B C
90 it, for] A; it—For B C
94 a] A; an B C
99 Sir,] A; Sir; B C
100 a] A; an B C
101 Generosity.—] A; Generosity—B C
102 Pocket Book,] A; Pocket-Book? B C
103 time we'll] A; time, we'll B C
105 Lodgings] A; Lodging B C
105 *Wilfull*] A; *Willful* B C
107 Door enquiring] A; Door, enquiring B C
109 here's] A; Here's B C
109 Sir.—] A; Sir. B C
110 'tis] A; 'Tis B C
111 hand] A; Hand B C
116 Respect upon] A; Respect, upon B C
117 you're] A; you are B C

118 discharged] A; discharg'd B C
122 I'm] A; I am B C
122 O,] A; Oh, B C
124 no,] A; No, B C
124 Child; your] A; Child, your B C
126 Wife, be] A; Wife be B C
127 Husband:] A; Husband—B C
128 Folly, be] A; Folly; be B C
129 kind; and] A; Kind, and B; kind, and C
130 Body] A; body B C
132 You *Silvia* in] A; you *Silvia*, in] B C
137 Liberty,] A; Liberty; B C
137 Wounds I'm] A; Wounds, I am B C
137 Gout,] A; Gout; B C
138 Liberty and hopes] A; Liberty, and Hopes B C
140 Year, but] A; Year—But B C
141 Beauty, my] A; Beauty my B C
141 Ambition] A; Ambition—B C
151 How!] B C; how! A
153 change?] A B; change; C
154 Constancy,] A; Constancy; B C
154 Outside] A; outside B C
155 Man,] A; Man; B C
157 romantick] A; Romantick B C
158 Adventures you] A; Adventures, you B C
159 side] A; Side B C
160 you] A; you'll B C
162 Friend, make] A; Friend; make B C
165 probable, I] A; probable I B C
166 yours, Madam] A; yours—Madam B C
169 you] A; You B C
171 my] A; My B C
173 I'm] A; I am B C
173 obedient.—] A; obedient—B C
174 Generation,—] A; Generation—B C
177 Sir, he] A; Sir—He B C
177 miracle; you] A; Miracle—You B C
178 too, that] A; too that B C
178 Captain] A; a Captain B C
179 *Dick*, he] A; Dick—he B C
181 *Jack*] A; *Jack*, B C
181 Bastard, ha, ha, ha,] A; Bastard —Ha, ha, ha, ha B C
181 pickled] A; pickl'd B C
183 yet, are] A; yet? Are B C
184 Privateer?] A; Privateer. B C
187 know.] B C; know A
188 Dear?] A; dear. B C
190 Probably I] A; Probably, I B C
192 Sweetheart] A B; Sweethart C
194 find *Mrs.* Rose has] A; find, Mrs. *Rose*, has B C
199 under-bred—but] A; under-bred, but B C
199 please I'll lye] A; please, I'll lie B C
202 you, or] A; you? or B C
203 her.] A; her? B C
206 wauns if] A; wauns! if B C
207 me, I'll desert] A; me I'll desart B C
208 that—My Dear,] A; that, my dear; B C
210 rais'd, at] A; rais'd at B C
211 my] A; My B C
216 *reward*] A; *Reward* B C
217 *train*] A; *Train* B C
218 *lasting*] A; *endless* B C

EPILOGUE

3 *Drury Lane*] A; Drury-Lane B C
8 Corps] B C; Corp'*s* A
9 do's] A; does B C
14 Schellenberg] A; Schellenbergh B C
17 *Stages*,] A; *Stages*. B C
26 Genius] A B; *genius* C
27 Defference] A; Deference B C
34 to Morrow] A; to morrow B C
35 shou'd] A; should B C

COMMENTARY

TITLE

21 *Captique dolis, donisque coacti.* Captured with tricks and brought together [or urged on by] with gifts. But the quotation is derived from Virgil's *Aeneid* II, 196: *captique dolis lacrimisque coactis* i.e. captured with tricks and forced tears. (The version in the first edition *Captique Aeolis donisque coacti* is absurd.) Eric Rothstein, *George Farquhar*, pp. 132–3, suggests that the misquotation leads the reader to regard Troy's foolish trust and disarmament as testimony for the necessity of English armament, and a justification for Kite's stratagems, while the comparison between beleaguered Troy and beleaguered Thummas Appletree is so grotesque "as to indicate Farquhar's limited sympathy for the victims of recruitment".

EPISTLE DEDICATORY

Dedication The Wrekin] An isolated hill, the nearest of the Carador Hills to Shrewsbury, the county town of Salop or Shropshire.

10 Salop] Shropshire.

28 *puris Naturalibus*] In the natural state.

34 Mr. Rich] Christopher Rich (d. 1714) the theatrical manager and producer. He was oppressive to the actors and Colley Cibber's *Apology* gives a long account of Rich's quarrels with them when he was Manager of the Theatre Royal, Drury Lane.

37 Mr. Durfey's third night] The third night was the author's benefit. Thomas D'Urfey (1653–1723) had written *Wonders in the Sun*, or *The Kingdom of the Birds* which was first produced at the Queen's Theatre, Haymarket on 5 April, 1706. In this burlesque opera Gonzales and Diego are carried to the Kingdom of the birds. D'Urfey wrote songs, tales, satires, melodramas and farces.

40 a huge Flight of frightful Birds] A reference to D'Urfey's burlesque opera mentioned in previous note.

52 *Woodcocks*] Probably means dupes, as a woodcock is notoriously easy to snare.

58 The Duke of *Ormond*] James Butler (1665–1745) 2nd Duke of Ormond, who commanded the English and Dutch land forces against Spain in 1702. He and Sir George Rooke (in command of the fleet) were victors at Vigo on 20 April, 1702. In 1703 he became Lord Lieutenant of Ireland. He was kind to Farquhar on the latter's visit to Dublin in 1704, but did not give him the commission he had hoped to receive in 1706 or 1707. See next note for details.

58 The Earl of *Orrery*] Charles Boyle (1676–1731) fourth Earl of Orrery gave Farquhar a commission as Lieutenant in the regiment

of foot of which he was Colonel. The post was worth three shillings per day. Farquhar sold the commission in late 1706 or early 1707 to pay his debts (some, no doubt, incurred in his recruiting campaign) in the expectation that the Duke of Ormond would give him "the first company that became vacant".

PROLOGUE

16 *bold* Hector *slain*] Achilles, in Homer's *Iliad* kills Hector, son of Priam King of Troy. He married Andromache and was the father of Astyanax.

ACT I, SCENE I

6 the *Raven*] This inn, known as the Raven Hotel, was situated in Castle Street, Shrewsbury until 1964 when it was demolished. F. W. Woolworth and Company Limited then built a new store on the site. It is believed in Shrewsbury that Farquhar lived here while writing *The Recruiting Officer*. The inn was originally established in the sixteenth century (see A. J. Wright, "Around the Castle", *Shrewsbury Chronicle*, 7 April 1970.)

12 the Cap of Honour] a tall, pointed cap.

13 Tricker] trigger.

17 list] enlist.

20 Conjuration] spell laid by sorcery.

24 woundily] excessively.

27 *The Crown, or the Bed of Honour*] The badge of the Grenadier Guards, a crown over the Royal Cipher or Monogram.

29 the great Bed of *Ware*] This bed, eleven or twelve feet square and capable of holding twenty four people was at the Saracen's Head, an Inn in Ware, Hertfordshire. Shakespeare referred to it (in *Twelfth Night*) as did other Elizabethan dramatists, and, later, Byron (in *Don Juan*). It was moved to Rye House, near the Inn.

36 Wauns!] wounds, contraction of God's wounds.

73 *Danube*] Because Plume is supposed to have come from Germany and the Blenheim campaign. Hochstadt (or Blenheim) is on the Danube.

73 *Severn*] The river flows through Shropshire.

79 strong Man of *Kent*] William Joy, who called himself Samson, the strongman of Kent, leased Dorset Gardens Theatre in 1699.

117 the *Buss*] 's Hertogenbosch, or Bois le Duc, in northern Brabant.

123 a Chopping Boy] a vigorous, strapping boy.

124 set the mother ... the boy in mine] C. Stonehill, *The Complete Works of George Farquhar* (1930) p. 433 quotes J. Hill Burton, *Reign of Queen Anne* (1880), I, 205, who mentions an incident of 1711 in relation to this passage:

Her Majesty having been pleased to grant Tilton Minshull, a child, a commission of ensign ... in order for the support of his mother and family ... has likewise given him a furlough to be absent from his duty until further order.

184 capitulate] to treat or negotiate.

300 Pipe] winecask holding about half a ton, e.g. two hogsheads or 126

old wine gallons or 105 imperial gallons.

300 *Barcelona*] wine from Barcelona.

ACT I, SCENE II

5 Spleen] melancholia.

31 no Salt ... no Hart's-horn ... nor Wash] Silvia's contempt for cosmetics is unusual in a heroine of the time.

31 Hart's-horn] substance produced by calcining or rasping the horns of harts, then a source for ammonia.

42 *And there's a pleasure sure in being mad, Which none but madmen know*] She quotes from Dryden, *The Spanish Friar*, II, ii.

44 Quixote] The hero of Cervantes' satirical romance, *Don Quixote de la Mancha* (1605, 2nd part 1615).

87 Rakely] rake helly, rascally.

ACT II, SCENE I

3 the last War] The French war or the war of the English Succession (1689–97) ended by the Peace of Ryswick.

3 no Blood, nor Wounds ... Mouths] a reference to the officers' oaths.

5 play at Prison Bars] a boys' game. C. Stonehill *op. cit.*, p. 434 describes it as on a par with hide-and-seek, or perhaps 'prisoners' base'.

7 odsmylife] contraction for "God's my Life".

8 another Mareschal of *France*] Mareschal Tallard was captured at Blenheim on 13 August, 1704. He was buried at Nottingham. Mareschal Bonflers surrendered at Namur.

13 *Hochstet*] Hochstadt (Blenheim).

70 Lack-a-day. Alack the Day, an exclamation of surprise.

ACT II, SCENE II

11 punctual] punctilious.

24 a Captain ... twelve hundred Pound a year!] An infantry captain was then paid about a hundred pound a year.

31 Cornishes] cornices.

34 *Habeas Corpus*] habeas corpus, a writ enforced by the Habeas Corpus Act of 1679, requiring the production in court of the body of a person imprisoned in order that the legality of the imprisonment can be investigated.

34 *Terra Firma*] earth.

35 *Chelsea* or *Twitnam*] Chelsea or Twickenham, London suburbs.

41 Prince *Prettyman*] a character in Buckingham's play *The Rehearsal* (1671). W. Archer comments that the character in that play who was torn between love and honour (in III, V) was Prince Volscurs. L. A. Strauss, in his edition of 1904 remarks that Farquhar makes the same mistake in one of his letters in *Love and Business*.

46 a Pad] an easy paced horse, a road horse.

121 a hank upon her Pride] a hold or power of restraint over her pride.

ACT II, SCENE III

4 *Over the hills*] See J. Genest, *An Account of the English Stage*, II, 340; 'On September 16, 1706, the Recruiting Officer was acted at Bath—several persons of quality were present—the news of the victory gained by the Duke of Savoy and Prince Eugene, reached

Bath that day—Eastcourt (the actor) added to the song in the Second Act—

'The noble Captain Prince Eugene
Has beat up French, Orleans and Marsin,
And march'd up and reliev'd Turin,
. . . Over the hills and far away.'

17 Wauns] wounds, contraction of God's wounds.

18 this pressing Act] The Mutiny and Impressment Acts of 1703, 1704 and 1705 which enabled Justices of the Peace to raise and levy such able-bodied men as had not 'any lawful calling or employment, or visible means for their maintenance and livelihood, to serve as soldiers'.

26 Queen of *England*] Queen Anne, who reigned from 1702–1714.

33 *two Broad Pieces*] Twenty shilling pieces from the reign of Charles I, worth £1 3s. 6d by 1706.

37 Posy] normally verse or motto on ring or brooch, here on the coin.

39 *Carolus*] Charles, the Latin name of the Monarch on the coins.

46 put them up] The mob accept the coins and by this trick are liable to enlistment.

59 Nab] a hat.

61 Vether] father.

79 St *Mary*'s . . . St *Chad*'s] St. Mary's Church, Shrewsbury, founded in the tenth century, and which still stands. It is architecturally interesting, having nave arcades with carved capitals of *c* 1200, the nave roof dating from the fifteenth century. The present great east window (from the old Grey Friars' church) is a "Jesse" window of English glass of *c* 1350. The church has a chiming clock with the usual four bells.

The present St. Chad's Church, Shrewsbury, was built between 1790–92, and is a magnificent Georgian building with circular nave and oval vestibule. A portion of the old St. Chad's Church (destroyed in 1788) to which Farquhar is referring here, which dated from 1571, remains, on a site supposed to be that of the Palace of the Prince of Powis, roughly south west of St. Mary's, the new St. Chad's Church being farther to the west beside the Quarry, Shrewsbury's public park.

116 Mayar] mayor.

139 A Month's mind] a continued intention (from the daily commemmoration of the dead for a month after death, with masses on the 3rd, 7th and 30th days).

154 I cod] rustic oath, egad.

165 duna] Mr Horden has quoted to the present editor an old piece of Shropshire lore:

Ye munna say wanna
It inna polite
Ye canna say "duna"
Cos that inna right.

ACT III, SCENE I

18 in her Smock] an unaffected, natural country girl (an obsolete phrase).

21 Song] This song was set to music by Leveridge; it was omitted in later editions; the tune was used in *The Beggar's Opera* (1728).

35 *die in your arms*] a pun on dying meaning (of men) to copulate.

45 break her Windows] a revenge

sometimes taken on whores. See Farquhar, *The Twin Rivals*, I, I, 27, for a similar use of the phrase.

50 Tit] girl, young person.

79 hast] haste.

79 liate] late.

83 Stracke] strike, or bushels: dry measure varying from 2 to 4 pecks.

84 higgle] haggle.

87 Groat] fourpence. Tucker Brook in his edition suggests 'I can make as much out of six as you can of half-a-dozen'.

88 Chapman] travelling salesman, hence bargainer, customer, or trader.

97 Ravelin] an outwork in fortification (with two faces jutting out to form a salient angle constructed beyond a main ditch or a main structure).

98 Palisado] A stake (set in rows to form a fence in a fortification); used by dragoons against cavalry charge.

125 Pistols] pistoles, Spanish coin or else Scottish twelve-pound piece (of William III period) worth about one pound.

132 halbard] halberd, a weapon like a spear with a battle axe head.

136 Truncheon] baton, mark of authority.

140 the Savoy] A liberty in the Strand, London, where there were, in addition to good houses and a prison, cheap lodgings.

172 the *Hungarians*] Allies of England against the Turks (who were allies of France at the time).

204 *Veni, vidi, vici*] Caesar's famous despatch "I came, I saw, I conquered" (his boastful account of his defeat of Pharnaces at the battle of Zela).

228 *Mor't de ma vie*] *Mort de ma vie*, French oath, "death of my life".

236 Landen] The battle of Landen, about 30 miles south east of Brussels which took place in July 1693. The Duke of Luxemburg defeated William III there.

252 *Chevaux de Frise*] projecting spikes laid to hinder opposing cavalry.

281 the Tombs and the Lions] The Tombs in Westminster Abbey and the lions kept in the Tower of London.

286 *Mechelin*] a fine lace made in Belgium.

291 Mangaree] probably Rose's error for orangeree, a snuff flavoured with orange blossom.

ACT III, SCENE II

5 Pinners] a headdress resembling a cap with long flaps pinned on each side and hanging over the cheeks of the wearer, or the flaps themselves.

39 Platoon] company of soldiers.

61 her Stove] English travellers often objected to the overheating of rooms on the continent. There may also be an English dislike of stoves as opposed to open fires expressed here. (But Goldsmith writes later of Dutch women who place small stoves under their skirts.)

62 *Bashaw*] earlier form of pasha.

88 Punk in the Pit] prostitute in the pit of the theatre.

90 *Tangerine*] a native of Tangiers, or the variety of orange which comes from there. Brazen, however, has earlier boasted of his service in Tangiers.

104 kneel, stoop and stand] a platoon was taught to fire from three positions.

191 *Holbourn*] Holborn, a district of London.

217 Caliber] calibre.

220 in effa ut flat] F fa ut, the fuller name of the note F which was sung to the syllable fa or ut as in one or other of the hexachords or imperfect scales to which it could belong (O.E.D.).

ACT IV, SCENE I

13 Tabor] a small drum.

78 the *West-Indies*] Then used as a penal settlement.

151 Centinel] private soldier.

254 Adso] contraction of adzoons, God's wounds.

ACT IV, SCENE II

3 Tide-waiter] customs official.

8 *Tycho, Ticho*] Tycho Brahe (1546–1601) a Danish astronomer who discovered a new star in the constellation Cassiopeia when in Germany in 1572. His chief work was *Astronomiae Instauratae Progymnasmata.*

20 *Copernicus*] Nicholas Copernicus (1473–1543) a Polish astronomer whose *De Revolutionibus Orbium* (1543) contained the theory that the earth and the other planets circled the sun.

31 *Forceps*] A smith's tongs, also obstetrical instrument.

33 the Signs] The twelve signs of the Zodiac, of which Kite remembers or knows only two, Leo and Sagittarius. Apart from "Forceps" the other names he gives are of five towns in Flanders (known to soldiers through the recent fighting there). Furns and Dixmunde are in West Flanders; Charleroi is 33 miles S. of Brussels, and Namur, on the confluence of the Sambre and Meuse lies farther to the S.W. of Brussels.

61 cheapning] cheapening, asking the price of.

78 *Tom . . .*] Tom tit, blue titmouse; Tom a Lincoln, Tom a Bedlam, a madman, a deranged person discharged from Bedlam, (see note on 1.) the asylum for the insane in London. Tom Fool, a buffoon.

163 Cleaver] butcher's chopper.

179 Claps] attacks of gonorrhoea.

240 *Cacodemon del fuego*] Demon from hell.

299 the Hour of Tea drinking] Tea was commonly taken in the morning.

321 the Chops of the Channel] the jaws or entrance to the English channel, approaching from the Atlantic.

236 Familiar] a demon supposed to attend at a witch's call, a spirit.

ACT V, SCENE II

21 *re infecta*] the act not yet accomplished.

32 Mr. Goose-cap] a reference to a Judge's wig.

63 *bien troussee*] neatly arranged.

64 Picket] piquet, a card game for two.

ACT V, SCENE III

40 till *Lent* be over] Marriages are not celebrated in Lent in the Roman Catholic Church and this custom may have prevailed generally.

ACT V, SCENE IV

5 two Sheep-stealers] convicted felons could be enlisted under the terms of the Impressment Act.

12 The Canonical Hour] The hours within which marriage could be legally performed in a parish church.

21 Privateer] an armed vessel, owned and officered by private persons holding commission from the government (called "Letters of Marque") who were authorised to use it against hostile nations, and especially in the capture of merchant shipping.

38 Specie] bullion.

67 ferry'd . . . Elysian fields] Charon, in Greek Mythology, ferried the dead across the Styx to Hades on payment of an obolus.

ACT V, SCENE V

30 sit by me] C. Stonehill *op. cit.*, p. 436 quotes J. Hill Burton, *op. cit.*, to the effect that regular army officers "were excluded from acting as Justices for the enrolment, and the Mutiny Acts and Articles of War were to be read over to the recruit before he was sworn and enrolled". Stonehill remarks that there is a touch of satire in the Justice's invitation to Plume, as showing that the restrictions of the Act were observed in the letter rather than in the spirit.

49 the *Cheshire* Round] a folk dance.

75 teeming] breeding.

89 the Act of Parliament] See note on 1. The Mutiny and Impressment Acts were 1 Anne, C. 16; 2 and 3 Anne C. 16 and C. 19.

139 Articles of War] See note on 1· (II, III).

146 Horse] wooden instrument for punishment of soldiers, known as the timber mare.

160 *Bedlam*] The lunatic hospital of St. Mary of Bethlehem, originally a priory. It was given to the City of London in 1547 and converted into a lunatic asylum.

ACT V, SCENE VI

10 Sharps] duelling swords.

187 Pickaroon] Picaroon, rogue, privateer, or private.

EPILOGUE

14 *Vigo*] The Spanish "Plate Fleet" was destroyed by the English and Dutch fleets at Vigo Bay in 1702.

14 *Schellenberg*] The Elector of Bavaria was defeated at Schellenberg by Marlborough and Prince Louis of Baden, on 2 July, 1704.

14 *Blenheim*] The battle took place at Hochstadt in Blenheim, on the Danube (N.W. of Augsburg) on 17 August, 1704. Marlborough and Prince Eugene defeated Franco-Bavarian forces there whereupon the French retreated west of the Rhine.

21 *Bononcini's*] Marc Antonio Bononcini (1675–1726) or his brother Giovanni Battista (1672–1750?) composed the music for *Il Trionfo di Camilla*, an opera translated by Owen MacSwiney and performed unsuccessfully at Drury Lane on 30 March, 1706. The sharply rhythmical music probably influenced Scarlatti in his composition of similar melodies.

25 Granadeer March] A march included in Playford's *Dancing Master* (1686), and not the *British Grenadiers*. The Epilogue is satirising a contemporary vogue for opera (especially French and Italian) in England.

25 Composure] composition.

28 the present Subscription] The opera was supported by subscription at the time.

29 Grand Alliance] A coalition against France, which included Holland and Leopold I in 1689. It subsequently was joined by England, Spain and Saxony; the purpose of the coalition was to prevent the Union of the French and Spanish crowns and to remove France from the Low countries.

BIBLIOGRAPHY

I. Works by Farquhar

A. COLLECTED WORKS

The Comedies of Mr. George Farquhar. London [1707]; [1710?]; 1711; 1714; 1718; 1721; 1728; 1736 (as *The Dramatick Works*, the 7th edition in 2 vols.).

The Works of the late Ingenious Mr. George Farquhar: containing all his Poems, Letters, Essays, and Comedies published during his lifetime. London [1711]; 1711 (2nd edition); 1714 (3rd edition); 1718; 1721; 1728 (6th edition); 1736 (7th edition); 1742 (8th edition); 1760 (9th edition); 1772 (10th edition); in 2 vols; 1775.

The Works. Dublin 1773 2 vols.

The Works, containing *The Life* by T. Wilkes, 3 vols. Dublin 1775.

The Dramatic Works of Wycherley, Congreve, Vanbrugh and Farquhar, ed. Leigh Hunt. London 1840.

The Dramatic Works of George Farquhar, ed. A. C. Ewald, 2 vols. London 1892.

The Complete Works of George Farquhar, ed. C. Stonehill, 2 vols. London (Nonesuch Press, Bloomsbury) 1930.

B. SELECTIONS

George Farquhar (4 plays) ed. W. Archer in the Mermaid Series. London (Benn) 1906; reissued 1949, 1959.

A Discourse upon Comedy, The Recruiting Officer and The Beaux Stratagem, ed. Louis A. Strauss. The Belles Lettres Series, Boston (D. C. Heath) 1914.

Representative English Comedies, ed. Charles Mills Gayley and Alwin Thaler. New York (Macmillan); London (Macmillan) 1936. This contains *The Recruiting Officer*, ed. Tucker Brooke.

C. THE RECRUITING OFFICER

The Recruiting Officer. London 1706; 1706 (2nd edition, corrected); 1706; 1707[?]; 1711; 1714 (the 5th edition); 1720; 1721; 1723; 1728; 1733; 1736; 1746; 1752; 1764; 1770; 1771; 1776; 1778; 1786; and 1877[?]. Other editions appeared in 1760; 1772; 1774; 1807; 1822; 1877 and 1885. Dublin 1722; 1727; 1732; 1741; 1751; 1765; 1768; 1786 and 1877[?]. Belfast 1773. Edinburgh 1759; 1768. An Apollo Press Edinburgh edition (for Bell, London) was published in 1782 (with remarks by Mrs. Inchbald). Boston 1822. *The Recruiting Officer* was edited (with a note on the author and the play) by Sir Edmund Gosse 1926, by Kenneth Tynan (Rupert Hart-Davis, 1965), by Michael Shugrue (University of Nebraska Press, 1965 and Edward Arnold, 1966) and by E. R. Wood (Heinemann Educational, 1969).

D. TRANSLATIONS AND ADAPTATIONS

Der Werboffizier, ein Lustspiel in Fünf Aufzugen von George Farquhar (Translated by George Heinrich Michaelis) in *Englisches Theater* (vol. 1), by Christian Heinrich Schmid, Dantzig and Leipzig 1772.

Die Werber (adaptation by G. Stephanie) Vienna 1778.

L'Officier en Recrutement translated by F. N. V. Campenon, in *Chefs d'oeuvres du Theâtre Anglais* V, Paris, 1823.

Ringen. Lystspil i Fire Akter efter Farquhar og Schrøder. Copenhagen 1868.

Pauken und Trompeten. An adaptation by Bertold Brecht, in collaboration with B. Besson and E. Hauptmann. Berlin 1955.

II. BIOGRAPHY AND CRITICISM

1. *The Eighteenth Century*

BEDFORD, ARTHUR, *The Evil and Danger of Stage Plays*. London 1706.

CHETWOOD, W. R., *A General History of the Stage*. London 1749.

"Mr. George Farquhar" in *The British Theatre*, pp. 129–31. London 1750.

CIBBER, COLLEY, *An Apology for the Life of Mr. Colley Cibber, Comedian . . . Written by Himself*. London 1740.

See also: *The Laureat or, the Right Side of Colley Cibber Esq*. London 1740.

CURLL, E., *The Life of that Eminent Comedian Robert Wilkes, Esq*. London 1733.

EGERTON, WILLIAM, *Some Memoirs of Mrs Anne Oldfield*. London 1731.

O'BRYAN, DANIEL, *Authentic Memoirs; or the Life and Character of . . . Mr. Robert Wilkes*. London 1732.

WILKES, THOMAS, "The Life of George Farquhar" in *The Works*. Dublin 1775.

2. *The Nineteenth Century*

GENEST, JOHN, *An Account of the English Stage*. London 1832.

GOSSE, EDMUND, *A History of Eighteenth Century Literature*, London (Macmillan) 1889

Gossip in a Library, London (Heinemann) 1891.

GUINEY, LOUISE IMOGEN, *A Little English Gallery*. New York 1894.

HARWOOD, THOMAS, *The History and Antiquities of the Church and City of Lichfield*. Gloucester 1806.

HAZLITT, W., "On Wycherley, Congreve, Vanbrugh and Farquhar" in *Lectures on the English Comic Writers*. London 1819.

LAMB, CHARLES, "On the Artificial Comedy of the Last Century" in *Essays of Elia*. London 1823.

THACKERAY, W. M., *The English Humourists of the Eighteenth Century*. London 1853.

WARD, A. W., *A History of English Dramatic Literature to the Death of Queen Anne* (3 vols.). London 1899

3. *The Twentieth Century*

ARCHER, W., *The Old Drama and the New*. London (Heinemann) 1923.

AVERY, EMMETT L., *The London Stage 1660–1800*. Part Two 1700–1729, Carbondale, Illinois 1960.

BERMAN, RONALD. "The Comedy of Reason" in *Texas Studies in Literature and Language*, VII (1965), pp. 161–8.

BERNBAUM, E., *The Drama of Sensibility*. Boston and London (Ginn and Co.) 1915.

BOAS, F. S., *An Introduction to Eighteenth Century Drama*. Oxford (Clarendon Press) 1953.

CONNELY, WILLARD, *Young George Farquhar. The Restoration Drama at Twilight*. New York (Scribner's) 1930; London (Cassell) 1949

DOBRÉE, BONAMY, *Restoration Comedy*. Oxford (Clarendon Press), 1924.

—English Literature in the Early Eighteenth Century, 1700–1740 *Oxford History of English Literature*, Vol. VII Oxford (Clarendon Press) 1959

FARMER, A. J., *George Farquhar*, in *Writers and Their Work* series. London (Longmans, Green) 1966.

FUJIMARA, T. H., *The Restoration Comedy of Wit*. Princeton (Princeton U.P.) 1952.

HOUGH, ROBERT L., "Farquhar: 'The Recruiting Officer'" *N & Q* New Series I, November 1954.

—"An Error in 'The Recruiting Officer'" *N & Q* CXCVIII, August 1963.

KAVANAGH, PETER, "Farquhar", *The Times Literary Supplement*, 10 February, 1945.

—*The Irish Theatre*. Tralee (The Kerryman) 1946.

KRUTCH, J. W., *Comedy and Conscience after the Restoration*. New York (Columbia U.P.) 1924.

LAURENCE, W. J., "George Farquhar: Thomas Wilkes", *The Times Literary Supplement*, 26 June, 1930.

LYNCH, KATHLEEN M., *The Social Mode of Restoration Comedy*. New York (Macmillan) 1926.

NETTLETON, G. H., *English Drama of the Restoration and Eighteenth Century*. London (Macmillan) 1914; New York (Macmillan) 1932.

NICOLL, ALLARDYCE, *A History of English Drama*, I–II. Cambridge (Cambridge U.P.) 1924; 1952.

PALMER, J., *The Comedy of Manners*. London (Bell) 1913.

PERRY, H. T. E., *The Comic Spirit in Restoration Drama*. New Haven (Yale U.P.) 1925.

PYLE, FITZROY, "George Farquhar (1617–1707)", *Hermathena* XCII (1958), pp. 3–30.

ROBERTSON, J. G., "Lessing and Farquhar" *MLR*, II, 1907.

ROSENFELD, SYBIL, "Notes on *The Recruiting Officer*", *Theatre Notebook*, XVIII Winter 1934.

ROTHSTEIN, ERIC, *George Farquhar*. New York (Twayne Publishers, Inc.) 1967.

SCHMID, D., *George Farquhar, sein Leben und seine original Dramen.* Vienna (Braumüller) 1904.

SMITH, J. H., *The Gay Couple in Restoration Comedy.* Cambridge, Mass. (Harvard University Press) 1948.

SPINNER, K., "George Farquhar als Dramatiker" in *Schweizer Anglistische Arbeiten.* Berne (Francke Verlag) 1956.

SUTHERLAND, JAMES, "New Light on George Farquhar", *The Times Literary Supplement*, 6 March 1937.

WHIBLEY, CHARLES, "The Restoration Drama, II" *Cambridge History of English Literature* Vol. VIII, Cambridge (Cambridge U.P.) 1912.